Cassandra's

PSYCHIC PARTY
GAMES

Cassandra's
PSYCHIC PARTY
GAMES

PIATKUS

Visit the Piatkus website!

Piatkus publishes a wide range of best-selling fiction and non-fiction, including books on health, mind, body & spirit, sex, self-help, cookery, biography and the paranormal.

If you want to:
- read descriptions of our popular titles
- buy our books over the Internet
- take advantage of our special offers
- enter our monthly competition
- learn more about your favourite Piatkus authors

VISIT OUR WEBSITE AT: www.piatkus.co.uk

Copyright © 2005 by Cassandra Eason

First published in 2005 by
Piatkus Books Ltd
5 Windmill Street
London W1T 2JA
email: info@piatkus.co.uk

The moral right of the author has been asserted

A catalogue record for this book is available from the British Library

ISBN 0 7499 2635 X

Text design by Goldust Design
Edited by Krystyna Mayer
Illustrations by Megan Hess

This book has been printed on paper manufactured with respect for the environment using wood from managed sustainable resources

Printed and bound in Great Britain by
William Clowes Ltd, Beccles, Suffolk

CONTENTS

To my children Tom, Jade, Jack, Miranda and Bill,
who taught me how to play.

INTRODUCTION

People have always played games at celebrations and family or community gatherings. It is part of human nature to compete and test our skills against those of others in a friendly way. Many early games were based on mating rituals – like the ancient (and still played) Scandinavian labyrinth game in which young males skate down different pathways of an ice-labyrinth maze, competing to be first to rescue the maiden of spring waiting in the centre. In the more distant past the victor would make love with the maiden to promote the fertility of the land and the crops (hopefully on a furry waterproof blanket!).

In a European Midsummer game with Celtic and Gaelic origins, flaming fire wheels were rolled down hillsides by youths at Midsummer to celebrate the power of the sun at its height. The one whose wheel reached the bottom of the hill first was feted as the mock Sun King at the festival and enjoyed all the benefits of a solar deity at his height of potency with the village maidens.

Like our ancestors we still have parties at Christmas and Halloween and on New Year's Eve, and such activities were much loved as Victorian parlour games. Fortune telling about love and relationships has retained its popularity at social occasions over the centuries. Fortune-telling games were associated with seasonal high points when the dimensions between present and future were considered most fluid and so the future was easier to predict. But a good party is a good party, winter or summer, so the activities described in the following pages can be engaged in at any time and in any place where people gather to have a good time.

PARTICIPATION IN GAMES

Until the late 1950s and early 60s, when television became a focal point in many homes, parlour games were central to family social occasions, as were singsongs around the piano.

How much more fun participation is than standing around with drinks and nibbles making polite conversation with relative strangers, or sitting at obligatory intergenerational family events, being shown holiday videos or watching television programmes with canned laughter. It is so much fun to play and laugh as you did at children's parties, to shed inhibitions and shyness, and to really get to know your fellow partygoers. Instead of engaging in speculation about which office colleagues are sharing late-night one-to-ones, you can use the tried and tested fortune-telling methods in the book to discover who would like an extra-curricular encounter with you.

Whether you are gathered with family and friends, looking for love, entertaining business colleagues or meeting new people at large events, the games in this book are all about interaction on a level beyond normal social chat. They are also an excellent way of channelling rivalries or dispelling underlying tensions or awkwardness.

The book offers a wide selection of games, from Druidic apple bobbing to fast and furious card competitions where chance overlaps with the innate predictive powers we all possess but seldom use.

WHY PSYCHIC PARTY GAMES?

Many of the old party games originated in an age in which there were no sharp divisions between competition, prophecy and a touch of magic to fulfil the dreams and wishes we may not even consciously have acknowledged. The first playing cards and Tarot cards were used at the same time for games and divination. The Vikings were convinced that the results of games of chance revealed the will of the gods and so were an accurate guide to future action.

When we are relaxed and having a good time, the conscious barriers that keep our sensible but somewhat restricted mindsets firmly in the here and now slip away. At such times we become more intuitive, aware and connected. Moreover, once people gather together a collective psychically charged energy is generated. You may find yourself talking to a complete stranger in a meaningful personal way you normally reserve for your mother or best friend. Indeed, games that encourage quiet moments are as much a part of this collection as are ones that involve more robust antics.

BUT I'M NOT PSYCHIC!

Have you ever met someone new and instinctively known not to trust them although the outward signs and even the body language were on cue? You may have noticed that in these cases you're always proved right.

Do you ever phone your mother, sister or best friend because you are suddenly worried about them only to find the number engaged?

You find out that they are dialling your number at precisely the same moment to ask for your help or advice.

Can you recall being delayed by transport problems or a rearranged schedule in an unfamiliar city and out of the blue thinking about someone with whom you went to school or college? Then you suddenly see them walking towards you because they were staying unexpectedly at your hotel because of a similar change of plans, although previously you had not seen or thought of them for years.

Do you ever spontaneously recall an old flame or friend you've lost touch with, and then receive a phone call to say that they are unexpectedly in town?

Have you ever changed your travel plans for no logical reason and then discovered that you narrowly avoided a traffic pile-up or a major public transport delay that would have caused you to miss a meeting, plane or ferry?

If you have a young child you may have woken in the night although you were exhausted, only to hear the child a minute later stirring because they are unwell. You may have had an impulse to check on them and found that their blankets had fallen off or they had become entangled in a pyjama jacket. You also know instinctively whether your child is really ill or just wants a cuddle and reassurance.

Have you ever remembered something urgent you meant to ask your partner to buy – then they arrive home with it and say, 'I thought you asked me to get it'?

Do you ever dream about something totally absurd or unusual, only for it to happen the next day?

We all have these natural normal psychic powers – or as some people call them, enhanced intuitive awareness. The more you use them, even in party games, the more finely tuned and effective these gifts become.

HOW DO PSYCHIC POWERS WORK?

The left logical side of the brain, the logical words part, is essential, enabling us to organise, analyse and categorise experiences, to catch trains and to make decisions using the available information. But we are not just creatures of logic and indeed, the most successful people in business rely on hunches, feelings and intuitions.

In the right part of the brain, the here and now of the left hemisphere is supplemented by speculation on possibilities and potentials. It can draw on the automatic radar we all have that can access information not available to the conscious mind and physical senses. These what ifs and maybes may appear as images, feelings or impressions. This part of the mind is most easily accessed when we are relaxed and happy.

Therefore as well as being entertaining, *Psychic Party Games* will teach you a lot you didn't know about yourself and your fellow partygoers.

Psychic tests in laboratories tend to be dull and don't often produce spectacular results. In contrast, because you are having a good time at a party the psychic insights come naturally, often as a by-product of the social aspects – and can give startlingly accurate results.

YOUR POWERS

Let's look at just a few of the powers you already have, that will emerge again during parties. As a welcome by-product in your everyday life, your enhanced intuitive senses will make you more aware of the whole picture both at work and socially, and you will become better equipped to anticipate opportunities or hazards.

Clairvoyance

This means clear-seeing beyond the range of the physical eye whether at a distance or through an opaque container, and also seeing into the past – and even the future. A number of games in this book naturally bring out our innate clairvoyance, for example Psychic Pass the Parcel, a remote viewing game in which you have to guess just from holding the parcel as it is passed around what it contains (see page 67).

Telepathy

Telepathy is mind-to-mind communication, the ability to pass images or information using thought processes. It is probably the most widespread everyday paranormal process. It forms the basis of an intriguing image transference game in Can You Read My Mind? (see page 27). This is a card guessing game adapted from an established, but in my opinion quite dull experimental process based on telepathy or Zener pattern cards. At a party this mind linking will identify people with whom you share a psychic wavelength. Although they may be total strangers at the beginning of the party they usually became firm future friends.

Psychometry

This is the power of psychic touch and is another ability that most people tune into almost instantly. We all have sensitive psychic energy centres in our hands through which we can receive very accurate impressions. For example, in everyday life you may visit an elderly aunt who shows you the family treasures. When you pick up a particular antique ring or a gold watch and chain, you may instantly know its history. Moreover, you can tune into the details of the lives of people who once wore it, although you have been told nothing about them. Games like Guess My Aura (see page 46) and You Really Were an Awful Child (see page 57) reveal hidden aspects of other guests as you link into their energy fields and perhaps find out their hidden secrets.

Psychokinesis

Psychokinesis, the power to move objects usually by unconscious mind power, is the basis of all fortune-telling games – ancient and modern. For the cards or dominoes we pick or win, or the dice combinations we throw, are the ones that will answer questions about love, money or success. This mind power also guides L-rods to find something that is hidden in Psychic Treasure Hunt (see page 73). In the psychic version of Truth or Dare? (see page 62) psychokinesis ensures that each victim chooses the most appropriate dare, and additionally identifies by a movement hard to fake whether a player is trying to conceal the truth. In this game your unconscious mind moves your hand to choose from pre-written, face-down choices.

IS IT SPOOKY?

Psychic senses are just an extension of our physical senses. However, once we start to rationalise our thoughts it becomes harder to spontaneously access these extrasensory powers. That is why young children, teenagers whose identity and hormones are all over the place, and animals naturally and regularly display psychic abilities. Relax with a glass of wine and the abilities flow.

There are absolutely no spooky scary games here involving summoning up spirits or messing around with ouija boards – these can be dangerous to use both psychologically and psychically. All the games are positive and the powers you use come from your own mind and not from passing entities.

You don't need advice from me on ensuring that younger guests play only the gentler games and that children attend family parties where they can play relaxed games. If an adult becomes overly sensitive while playing a game (perhaps due to previous emotional trauma or because they've drunk too much alcohol), bring the game to a positive and gentle conclusion with a joke and lots of earthly reassurance. Make sure they have lots of carbohydrates and orange juice to ground them.

PSYCHIC PARTIES

In essence, psychic games can become part of any social occasion, from a black tie one to a family barbecue. However, psychic theme parties create a gathering with a difference.

You can hold psychic evenings at any time, but they are particularly good during the full or crescent moon, when guests can light candles, write wishes on paper and burn them in the flames.

A number of the games can be played outdoors either during the day or by candlelight and torchlight. You can also stay up all night on the longest day around 21 June (six months later in the southern hemisphere) and greet the sun from the local hilltop and have a dawn picnic.

For a psychic party at any time:

❋ Decorate the room with spooky black candles and light heady incense sticks with fragrances such as jasmine or sandalwood.

❋ Make CDs or tapes with magic themes in advance – 'I Put a Spell on You', 'Voodoo Woman', 'Devil in Disguise', etc.

❋ Be ingenious and create themed foods and tomato or cranberry juice-based punches. You are limited only by your imagination. If you raid children's party cookery books for ideas you can transport even the most world-weary sophisticate back to the nursery with blood-red, additive-filled jelly fights on a vampire night.

ABOUT THE GAMES

Each game is self-explanatory. At the beginning of every game there is a quick summary telling you what the game is about, the number of players and the kind of event it is best for. This enables you to assess if it is right for the event you have in mind. At the end of each game are listed related games so you can play similar games during the same evening if you wish.

Choose games according to how well guests know each another and how well acquainted they would like to be by the end of the party. With strangers or acquaintances, start with a game in which players can relax and talk to different people for a short time, like Astro Twins (see page 12). This is a good ice-breaker, where guests try to find people with compatible star signs, or best of all someone who shares their zodiacal viewpoint. More active games like the Archangel Wheel Game (see page14), where the forces of light have to overcome the fallen archangels, may be better for later in the evening, when everyone is mellow and less self-conscious. Vary the pace, following hectic games like Druidic Apple Bobbing (see page 125) with quieter ones like the Image Game (see page 3).

Make sure you have everything ready beforehand so there are no last-minute hitches, although usually guests are more than happy to improvise. Take time to explain the game and if necessary have a dummy run.

I have suggested follow-up activities for each game, sometimes developing the predictive aspect or offering a variation on the theme, so that those who are fascinated can try different but related psychic methods. Use your gut feelings as well as murmurs from the guests to assess when a game has run its course.

PARTY GAMES

IMAGE GAME

What is it?
A psychic game that enables you to understand the image you are projecting socially, romantically and in your work life. It also shows you how to improve your charisma by changing your name or signature by even a single letter.

Number of players
Any.

Event
An intimate game for close friends; also for family gatherings or teenage sleepovers, or after Sunday lunch. A quiet game that can be played in a very limited space.

ABOUT THE GAME

According to numerology, by choosing the precise name we use, psychologically and psychically, we create the impressions we desire and draw into our lives the kind of people and lifestyle we want. Often it is as simple as altering a single letter in your first name or adopting an abbreviated form of your name with which you feel comfortable.

Numerology as we use it today dates back to the sixth century BC, when the Greek philosopher and mathematician Pythagoras taught that each of the primary numbers (1 to 9) has different vibrations, and that these vibrations echo throughout the cosmos. Each name can be calculated numerologically and reflects the power of the sum total of all the numbers of the name when reduced to one of the primary numbers.

In this game you work with one or two other people to experiment creating the name/s that numerologically reflect not only how you would like to be seen by others, but also how you would like to feel inside.

EQUIPMENT

1. Copies of the chart below
According to how many people are playing.

1	2	3	4	5	6	7	8	9
A	B	C	D	E	F	G	H	I
J	K	L	M	N	O	P	Q	R
S	T	U	V	W	X	Y	Z	

2. Pens and paper

3. Calculators

For those who want to use them.

4. Incense sticks

Such as sandalwood, frankincense, orange or myrrh, for the follow-up activities.

5. Bowl of small, mixed crystals

If you want to do the follow-up activities.

> ### Game in a hurry
> **Draw the number values on a blackboard or white board where everyone can see them, plus keywords for each number from 1 to 9.**

HOW TO PLAY

✳ This is the procedure each player in the game should follow. Using the chart (where A, J and S represent 1, etc.), calculate the value of your first name (or the name you use in a social situation) to see what its number projects according to the list given in the results section. This will give you the information about your love life and social life.

✳ Write down the number values of the individual letters in the name, then add them together. Reduce the result by adding together the two digits of the number obtained to make a single prime number. For example, if your name numbers added up to 32, you would reduce the 32 further to 5 (3 + 2), and 5 would be your current personality number.

✳ In order to find your work personality traits you can also add the letters of any middle names and surname (or a name by which you are addressed at work) to see how different facets of your personality reflect numerologically in different situations.

✳ For now focus on what people call you at the party and the social/love implications. Then experiment changing different letters in your name until you get the meaning you want socially and romantically. Examples of what the numbers mean in connection with work are also given in the results (see below).

✳ Let's use the example of Lindsay, a 30-year-old single radio producer who would like to meet the man of her dreams, but always ends up sorting out the problems of the men she meets.

The present spelling of the name is L I N D S A Y, which gives: 3 + 9 + 5 + 4 + 1 + 1 + 7 = 30 and 3 + 0 = 3.

Three is the number of the Creator, dynamic, capable and strong. But Lindsay doesn't really want to be the strong one in love – she's had enough of lame ducks. She would like to be cherished and a woman of mystery.

She changes one letter in her name – the 'A' to an 'E', to give:

LINDSEY, which gives $3 + 9 + 5 + 4 + 1 + 5 + 7 = 34$ and $3 + 4 = 7$.

The number 7 is the number of the mystic, mysterious, unattainable, magical, and alluring person that she wants to be.

✳ Sometimes it won't be that easy and you'll have to play around for a while to get the right letter combination to project the number value you want.

✳ Check the personality traits in the list below, which apply equally to men and women. It is possible to change the emphasis in a current relationship for the better by projecting your new adopted number persona.

✳ Keep playing the game until your guests lose interest.

THE RESULTS

Here are the numerological meanings:

ONE The Innovator
Love and socially Always ready to go anywhere and do anything to have a good time; your relationships will never be dull or stagnant and you'll always be the first to try anything on offer.
Work Potentially a leader and great at working on your own initiative; harder for you to be a team member.

TWO The Negotiator

Love and socially Perfect number for settling down and possibly acquiring a ready-made family, or for nest-building; you'll get your own way by persuading others that they thought of an idea in the first place.

Work Good for troubleshooting roles and behind-the-scenes deals, but you won't always get much credit for your achievements.

THREE The Creator

Love and socially Artistic, flamboyant and theatrical – able to throw tantrums and get everyone running to grant your every whim.

Work You are inspirational and good at making any environment beautiful, but constantly change your mind and focus.

FOUR The Realist

Love and socially Happiest with love that grows from friendship or familiarity (the boy or girl next door); good at making the future happen step by step; definitely the archetypal *Brides and Homes* magazine material.

Work Rise to the top slowly but surely, with pension plans for a golden tomorrow.

FIVE The Voyager

Love and socially Need a travelling companion and free spirit as a lifetime mate to satisfy perpetually itchy feet (or at least provide two good holidays a year); any future offspring of yours will see the world from a baby carrier – and thrive on it.

Work Whether in the travel industry, making connections overseas or relocating, this is the number of limitless possibilities. The world could be your oyster.

SIX The Nurturer

Love and socially You'll never be alone and with you the right partner will blossom and flourish through your gentleness. Your home will always be full of visitors, friends, animals and extended family, and you will live in total harmony, if not riches.

Work Working with people is your forte and will energise you and offer you total job satisfaction.

SEVEN The Mystic

Love and socially Unpredictable, exotic, unknowable you, to be cherished, adored and yet always keep your secrets; you will be loved either by someone strong and worldly, or by another mystic with whom you will reach great emotional heights.

Work You will thrive on being involved in anything alternative or non-mainstream, clairvoyance, health and healing – or you may be a scholar of ancient mysteries.

EIGHT The Entrepreneur

Love and socially Love and work relationships are often entwined. You are a speculator and powerful person, destined for great riches one day. You and your future partner may well set up your own business, invest in property or become Mississippi paddle-boat gamblers. You'll ride the financial roller coaster together.

Work Definitely anything to do with money or investment or a high-tech career; opportunities will follow fast and you will have to run to keep up with Lady Luck.

NINE The Perfectionist

Love and socially Love, like life, will be perfectly coordinated and smooth running – ideal mate, ideal family if you want one, ideal home, living the dream and making sure that whatever you do you enjoy the best within your means – even if you have to work on a cruise liner to enjoy your around the world trip.

Work Be prepared to work 24/7 to get the job you want on the career path you seek to conquer. To others your rise will seem effortless.

TIPS Experiment with a variety of names and even job titles in different roles as you can mix and match and get the best of both worlds – for example, a 9 at work and a 7 in love.

Consult closely with others during the game as they may spot potentials you have missed.

FOLLOW-UP ACTIVITIES

In all the best magical traditions of the past, practitioners chose a numerologically appropriate secret power name or names, such as Isis or Ariadne of the Waves. They would recite this name nine times in their minds before an important event – or write the name nine times in incense smoke over a lucky pendant or charm that they carried with them.

Have fun creating your power name or names but do not tell anyone what they are. Using incense sticks, write your power name in smoke over personal items nine times.

If you don't have any suitable personal items, take a small crystal from the bowl of mixed crystals to empower and carry as a lucky charm. Clear or sparkling crystals are energising and joyful; soft, muted shades are gentle; and rich, opaque colours are strong and dynamic. If in doubt close your eyes and take a crystal from the bowl and that will be the right one for you.

If you have enjoyed this game you may also like to try:
What's My Future? (see page 19)
Domino Speculation Power Game (see page 98)
Who Will Be a Millionaire First? (see page 107)

ASTRO TWINS

What is it?
An ice-breaking conversational game where strangers and acquaintances use their birth signs as a way of getting to know each another better – with the ultimate aim of meeting an Astrological Twin or at least someone who shares their Zodiac sign.

Number of players
As many as possible.

Event
Anywhere guests have not met before, whether in business or socially; good for launch parties and corporate events; also big post-wedding parties or singles' evenings.

ABOUT THE GAME

This is a psychic theme game rather than one that tests skills. The idea is to talk to as many people as possible in two-minute bursts to ascertain whether you share birthdays/birth signs, and if not, whether you are astrologically compatible.

Astrological Twins are defined as two unrelated people born on the same day, at the same hour, in the same world region, and who therefore share almost identical astrological charts. True Astrological Twins in the strictest definition are born on the same day within 30 minutes of each other within a radius of 500 miles. But people are also counted as 'twins' if they are born within 90 minutes of each other within a radius of 1,000 miles, or where one or both of the twins has an unknown time of birth, but is within the 1,000-mile world zone.

Because of this there are many recorded instances of Astrological Twins sharing the same interests, career choices and major life changes. It is unlikely that you will find an Astrological Twin at a party, but we can relate closely to others who share our birth sign, and may have an almost instant love-hate relationship with those born under other birth signs. This game offers the chance to get to know a wide variety of other guests by initiating conversation about the almost universal fascination with birth signs and horoscopes and discovering as many similarities/differences as possible in two minutes.

Game in a hurry
All happening pretty fast anyway.

EQUIPMENT

1. Chart of astrological compatibilities and birth sign qualities list (one of each for each player)

See page 213 for birth sign qualities list.

ASTROLOGICAL COMPATIBILITIES

The closer to your birthday the other person is, either within the same sign or occasionally just over the cusp (in the sign before or after yours) the closer the similarities in your personality and lifestyle. Of course, other astrological factors, such as the ascendant sign and moon at birth, also play a part.

Sign	Harmonious with	Difficult/ defensive with	Tumultuous but exciting with
Aries	Aries, Taurus, Gemini, Leo, Sagittarius, Aquarius and Pisces	Cancer, Libra (the opposing sign) and Capricorn	Virgo and Scorpio
Taurus	Taurus, Gemini, Cancer, Virgo, Capricorn, Pisces and Aries	Leo, Scorpio (the opposing sign) and Aquarius	Libra and Sagittarius

Sign	Harmonious with	Difficult/ defensive with	Tumultuous but exciting with
Gemini	Gemini, Cancer, Leo, Libra, Aquarius, Aries and Taurus	Virgo, Sagittarius (the opposing sign) and Pisces	Scorpio and Capricorn
Cancer	Cancer, Leo, Virgo, Scorpio, Pisces, Taurus and Gemini	Libra, Capricorn (the opposing sign) and Aries	Sagittarius and Aquarius
Leo	Leo, Virgo, Libra, Sagittarius, Aries, Gemini and Cancer	Scorpio, Aquarius (the opposing sign) and Taurus	Capricorn and Pisces
Virgo	Virgo, Libra, Scorpio, Capricorn Taurus, Cancer and Leo	Sagittarius, Pisces (the opposing sign) and Gemini	Aquarius and Aries
Libra	Libra, Scorpio, Sagittarius, Aquarius, Gemini, Leo and Virgo	Capricorn, Aries (the opposing sign) and Cancer	Pisces and Taurus

Sign	Harmonious with	Difficult/ defensive with	Tumultuous but exciting with
Scorpio	Scorpio, Sagittarius, Capricorn, Pisces, Cancer, Virgo and Libra	Aquarius, Taurus (the opposing sign) and Leo	Aries and Gemini
Sagittarius	Sagittarius, Capricorn, Aquarius, Aries, Leo, Libra and Scorpio	Pisces, Gemini (the opposing sign) and Virgo	Taurus and Cancer
Capricorn	Capricorn, Aquarius, Pisces, Taurus, Virgo, Scorpio and Sagittarius	Aries, Cancer (the opposing sign) and Libra	Gemini and Leo
Aquarius	Aquarius, Pisces, Aries, Gemini, Libra, Sagittarius and Capricorn	Taurus, Leo (the opposing sign) and Scorpio	Cancer and Virgo
Pisces	Pisces, Aries, Taurus, Cancer, Scorpio, and Capricorn	Gemini, Virgo (the opposing sign) and Sagittarius	Leo, Libra and Aquarius

2. Bell or buzzer
This can be sounded every two minutes as a signal to move on to the next person.

3. Clock
For timing.

4. Pencil and paper for each player

HOW TO PLAY

* Give everyone their list of birth sign qualities and astrological compatibilities chart well before the game so they can have a quick look if they are unfamiliar with basic astrological material.

* One person needs to be in charge of the timer and buzzer or bell.

* When the game begins each person should pair with the person standing nearest to them, and when the bell or buzzer sounds they must quiz each other about their basic astrological characteristics. For example: 'Do you often change your mind?' (Gemini), or 'Are you cautious with money' (Capricorn).

* After a couple of questions from both people in the pair, each should make a guess as to the birth sign of the other. They then exchange birth dates in order to ascertain astrological compatibility and to see if they are twins or even a near miss.

* Guests can check their charts if they forget compatibilities and

can then continue to chat about their horoscopes until the two minutes are up.

※ Guests should note names, birth dates and compatibilities using the pens and paper provided.

※ The exercise should then be repeated with a different person every two minutes (allowing a short time between each turn to change partners).

※ The game continues until interest wanes or all the guests have interviewed each another.

THE RESULTS

Everyone can check who they are the most compatible with and return for a longer chat with that person. They may also like to talk to a person with whom there is potentially a tumultuous but exciting link.

TIPS The participants should use their intuition when talking to new people as time is very short.

They shouldn't waste their two minutes on small talk or flirting – they can always return later in the evening to develop the connections.

FOLLOW-UP ACTIVITIES

Participants can find someone with their polar or opposing sign: Aries/Libra, Taurus/Scorpio, Gemini/Sagittarius, Cancer/Capricorn, Leo/Aquarius, Virgo/Pisces.

They can chat about their pet hates and likes and may find that they have a very stimulating conversation. Remember the old adage – opposites can attract.

If you have enjoyed this game you may also like to try:
Guess My Aura (see page 46)
Can You Read My Mind? (page 27)
Past Life Game (see page 20)

PAST LIFE GAME

What is it?
A potentially mind-blowing but fun group game that explores connections between the players in past times and worlds.

Number of players
Two to twelve.

Event
Intimate late night times when the lights are low; good for lovers alone or for a group of close friends after supper; also for student and dating parties.

ABOUT THE GAME

We do not know whether we have lived before or whether we tap into past worlds through some genetic memory. A number of experts maintain that modern humans first came out of East Africa more than a million years ago. Whatever our collective origins, we are all related (albeit distantly) to other humans. Therefore it may be possible for us to tap into the collective memory pool, called by the psychotherapist Jung the 'collective unconscious', and share visions of other worlds.

There is, however, also a theory that groups of souls are naturally connected and meet up in different lifetimes in which they have different roles, according to the lessons to be learned. Therefore a group of close friends or two lovers (or sometimes people who are drawn together, for example at a party) may share past experiences. These can be recalled in a relaxed atmosphere.

Even if this sounds unlikely we can all access the past through our innate clairvoyant powers and so can tap into a collective scene from the past through shared intimacy. Music, soft light and fragrance are ways of carrying the mind beyond the conscious to a deeper, more spontaneous level that can access buried psychic material.

EQUIPMENT

1. Two or three incense sticks
These should be sandalwood, frankincense or any floral variety and should be set around the room in containers to collect the ash.

2. Scented candles or tea lights
These should be rose, beeswax or lavender and there should be enough to illuminate the room.

3. Large beeswax candle in a deep holder
A glass with sand inside makes a good holder and this candle should act as a focus in the centre of the room.

4. Very soft background music
Gregorian chants, choral music, harpsichord and flutes, relaxation music or Buddhist chants are all good.

5. Dark crystal (optional)
This is passed around and used to connect individuals with a collective past. An amethyst or smoky quartz sphere, round crystal or small geode is ideal. If not, use a dark crystal egg or large, round dark stone. It can double as a protective charm in your work space after the party.

HOW TO PLAY

* Before the party light the incense and the background and central candles.

* Draw any curtains to exclude external light and make sure all phones are switched off. Bleeping and past lives do not mix well.

* Before beginning, warn any potential jokers not to mess about

with strange voices and not to try and spook anyone or the whole thing just won't work. Explain that you are not calling up spirits or ghosts, just looking into the past as though on a DVD.

* Put on the music so it is just audible. Sit in a circle in the candlelit room, or if only two of you are playing, sit across a table with the large candle between you.

* As the hostess, you hold the crystal and start the game.

* Each person present should initially focus on establishing a quiet, regular breathing pattern and picture the shadows around the central candle changing and forming images of other places and other times.

* After two or three minutes, look into the candle flame and ask very softly and slowly: 'When was it I last saw you? Come to me through mists of time and let me walk once more familiar pathways.'(You can teach the other players the mantra in advance.)

* You should then describe just one or two features of the earlier world that spontaneously appears in your mind or around the candle flame. For example, you might see an open fireplace, a sunny hillside or a market place. It is important that you don't create or imagine a scene but let your voice speak spontaneously.

* Pass the crystal or stone to the person on your left, who should then ask: 'When was it I last saw you? Come to me through mists of time and let me walk once more familiar pathways.'

* They should, without thinking or pausing, add some more details that they also see and then hand the crystal on to the person on their left.

* As each person says the mantra and adds details, everyone else should try to picture the scene building up around the candle flame into the party room.

* There invariably comes a point where at least some people in the circle can externally 'see' the past world around them and may see other guests in different clothes or looking different. This is quite normal and can be discussed afterwards. Don't worry if the participants' voices change slightly as the game progresses. No one is being taken over by spirits. It is just a connection with the past being expressed as the two dimensions meet. It may feel a little cold and the candle may flicker, but this is quite normal as we look across time.

* After you have been around the circle of guests once, put the crystal aside and say that people should add details aloud when they wish without beginning with the mantra.

* Generally the experience draws to a natural conclusion and people fall silent. No one will be in a trance, but if you have anyone very sensitive present and they start to get anxious or see anything that is not happy, this is the point when you should steer the game to a close.

* Towards the end of the game, pick up the crystal once more and

say: 'So we leave the past in peace and return to our present lives and loves here and now, recalling only what was good and joyful.'

✳ Then count slowly, regularly and quietly aloud from ten to one and say: 'And now we are home.'

THE RESULTS

Sit quietly in the candlelight for a few minutes and then initiate a discussion, as people usually recall far more at this point than they reported during the game. See if you can identify the period from clues in clothing, buildings, ships, etc., and pinpoint a location.

TIPS As soon as you (or the other participants) are given the crystal or stone, let your voice speak and don't rationalise or monitor what you are saying.

Focus on the central candle flame throughout the game (blinking or closing your eyes whenever necessary).

Try to picture the images other people are creating without questioning them in your mind or out loud (you can discuss them afterwards).

FOLLOW-UP ACTIVITIES

Talk about past-life dreams and experiences generally, déjà vu experienced in old places and any feelings of being drawn to particular lands or periods. Plan a trip to a museum, old house or site that has links to the period experienced in the game.

If you have enjoyed this game, you may also like to try:
Guess My Dark Secret (see page 81)
Halloween Party Games (see pages 123–144)
New Year Party Games (see pages 169–194)

CAN YOU READ MY MIND?

What is it?
A fun telepathy game to test psychic compatibilities with friends or even strangers.

Number of players
Four to ten, but really no maximum as long as you have an even number and a set of cards per pair of people.

Event
Ideal for breaking the ice at mixed gatherings or for quiet, fun evenings at home with family and friends.

ABOUT THE GAME

This card game tests your telepathic ability to read the mind of another person and for them to tune in psychically to you. The better the joint total score of correct guesses with a particular person, the more compatibility there is between you and that partner. High scores can happen even with total strangers.

By playing the game with different people you can find your party soul mate for the evening, or maybe even more than one person who is in tune with you.

EQUIPMENT

1. Card sets

There are five different card designs in all, each showing a different party symbol. Each set has five of each design, making up 25 cards.

The card sets are really quick to make using ready-made, small, blank white cards and a felt-tip pen. The colours are optional and you can substitute five party symbols of your own choice for the ones below if you wish.

The suggested symbols are:

Card 1 Balloon with curly string (red)
Card 2 Bottle of wine (green)
Card 3 Cake with five candles (purple)
Card 4 Mask like those worn at masked balls (blue)
Card 5 Party hat or crown (orange)

The 25 cards should be of identical shape and size – about the size of a small playing card, and the backs of the cards should be left blank. If you laminate the card sets you can keep them for other parties.

2. Score sheet for each partnership's test scores

On each sheet, you need two columns and a space at the top of each column to note the names of the two players in the game. Below each name write the numbers from 1 to 25. I have shown an example below although I have just drawn the first five rows to give you the idea.

Name	Name
Guess	Guess
1	1
2	2
3	3
4	4
5	5

3. Compatibility card

Each person needs a piece of paper or a blank postcard on which to note the different partnership scores so that at the end they can see with whom they scored the highest number of correct guesses (and who therefore they are most psychically linked with).

HOW TO PLAY

✳ Each person needs to choose an initial partner. If possible this should be someone that they do not already know.

✳ In each pair, one person agrees to act as sender (or transmitter) of the telepathic images on the cards, while the other acts as receiver of the telepathic thoughts. The sender is also responsible for recording the results.

✳ Both look at the card pack and familiarise themselves with the images. If they can share jokes about the drawings they will kick-start the connection between them.

✳ The sender takes the pair's card set (of 25) and the receiver sits with their back to the sender.

✳ The sender shuffles or mixes the pack well and sets the pack of cards in a pile face down in front of him. He will turn them face up, one at a time.

* When he is ready the sender says 'Ready' followed by 'Now' as he turns the first card over.

* The receiver names aloud the first card turned over and the sender enters a tick or cross next to Number 1 in the first column on the score sheet.

* Speed is of the essence. The sender must set the pace, working as fast as possible to transmit the telepathic images one after the other without pause. He says 'Now' before he turns each card. The card turning and transmitting rate should average about ten seconds per card, plus an extra five seconds maximum for the receiver to make the guess and the sender to mark the tick or cross in the correct box on the score sheet.

* When all 25 cards have been dealt face up by the sender and the receiver's guesses have been made and recorded, the sender and receiver change roles (without counting the ticks).

* They play the game once more in their new roles.

* Afterwards the sender and receiver can count the total number of ticks over the two games to see how many correct guesses in total between them were made, regardless of who was transmitting at the time. This number gives the pair their psychic compatibility score. The maximum number would be 50 correct guesses, which is unheard of.

* The score sheet should be discarded but partners should note their compatibility ratings with each other.

* Each individual then chooses a new partner and the pair take a new partnership score sheet until each guest has worked with as many people as possible before you, as the party host, call a halt to the game.

* For each new partnership the individual acts as sender for one game and receiver for one game.

* At the end, everyone should contact the person with whom they have the highest compatibility score. This is the highest number of correct answers in one of the partnerships.

* At the end when you have called a halt to the name (about 20 minutes is usually enough unless people are really absorbed) you can explain the results.

THE RESULTS

If you play the game with a partner (once as sender, once as receiver), a compatibility rating of ten or lower is simply chance. Any compatibility rating over ten indicates a psychic connection.

The compatibility strengthens the more correct guesses there are, so of a potential 50 correct, if John and Sue got 13 guesses correct and John and Alison got 15, then John and Alison are more psychically compatible than John is with Sue, However, there is still a psychic spark between John and Sue. If Alison and Anne get 16 correct guesses together out of a possible 50 they are definitely telepathically linked.

The link gets stronger the more correct guesses a partnership makes. Twenty correct guesses out of 50 and there is definitely a lot in common; 30 and there will be lots of similarities in the two players' lives even if they have never met before. Forty is pretty amazing and more than that we are talking twin souls.

TIPS The more relaxed people are the better chance they have of making an extrasensory connection, so parties are ideal for telepathic games.

Participants shouldn't try to guess the answers. The less hard they try the more their spontaneous psychic powers will kick in.

If a number of people are playing, ensure that you have plenty of corners and chairs/cushions so the pairs can go off to work together.

FOLLOW-UP ACTIVITIES

If any of the participants get anything over ten correct guesses, then it's worth them getting to know the people they match with psychic-ally. They should ask if they have birth or elemental signs, ages, families and interests in common.

If you and the other participants already know each other don't be surprised if you (and they) score highly with someone you thought you disliked. It may be the psychic similarity that makes you rub each other up the wrong way. This is a good chance to get to know each other amicably.

Iffy scores for established couples are not omens of divorce. Play a game or two more to see if the compatibility improves. If not, maybe it's a signal to spend more time together (not just playing cards), to revive the original spark that drew you together. Perhaps you should leave the party early together and consign your potential psychic soul mates to your dreams.

If the group is small you might like to play more than two games together. If you play four in a partnership (two as sender and two as receiver), then any score over 20 out of 100 (4 lots of 25 guesses) shows a link. A score of over 28 starts to get spooky.

If you go for the marathon and play ten games with the same partner (five as sender and five as receiver) then over 50 guesses out of 250 is a sign of psychic links; if it is 63 out of 250 you may want to meet again after the party.

If you have enjoyed this game you may also like to try:
Astro Twins (see page 12)
Psychic Pass the Parcel (see page 67)
Pass the Crystal Ball (see page 86)

I SPY WITH MY CLAIRVOYANT EYE

What is it?
A relaxed telepathic drawing game, based on the ability to transfer images from one mind to another.

Number of players
A minimum of six.

Event
Intergenerational and suitable for all kinds of parties; loved by men and children of all ages – although men usually find that they are far outmatched by young children.

ABOUT THE GAME

Telepathy or mind-to-mind communication is common between relations, close friends and lovers because their thought patterns have spontaneously become synchronised over time. The better you know the people you play with the more successful generally you are. However, the game works well even with strangers, especially at parties where everyone is relaxed.

As is shown in the card game Can You Read My Mind? (see page 27), it has been discovered that telepathic information is most easily transmitted in the form of images.

In this game one person acts as transmitter and creates a simple line image on paper. By visualising the line drawing three-dimensionally in its natural context, the transmitter can convey the image into the minds of other players. They then reproduce what they perceive in the form of a simple line drawing on paper.

EQUIPMENT

1. Black pens or crayons

2. Small pad of paper for each player

3. Clock or watch with a second hand

HOW TO PLAY

* All the players sit in a circle or around a table.

* One person volunteers to act as the transmitter for the first game and leaves the table but stays in the room.

* He or she draws an image on their pad as fast as possible, covers it up and returns to the circle.

* The transmitter visualises the object in context and if possible endows the image with emotion, by perhaps visualising something funny about the pictured scene.

* The transmitter places the clock or watch in front of them.

* Everyone stares at the transmitter. They imagine a television screen in their own minds upon which the scene with the clear black outline of the chosen image in the centre appears in 3D.

* Each person draws the image as fast as possible.

* After about a minute the transmitter says 'stop' and everyone reveals their drawings.

* The person whose drawing is most like the transmitter's or features the most similar object is the winner.

* Results can be briefly discussed, then the winner becomes the next transmitter and also keeps time.

* If no one draws anything remotely like the image the person

sitting to the left of the first transmitter draws the second image, again leaving the table.

❋ The game continues until people have had enough.

THE RESULTS

The overall winner is the one with the most correct guesses, but any correct guess is very impressive. In the course of several games you may notice that one person, usually someone very relaxed and open, transmits most easily to other people. Very logical people can get frustrated if, for example, a small child next to them gets 100 per cent guesses right.

TIPS If any players can't see an image in their minds, they should let their minds go blank and allow their hands to draw objects without consciously thinking about what they are drawing.

The essence is speed as once people start trying to rationalise, telepathy is less effective.

FOLLOW-UP ACTIVITIES

These are endless and you can move on to writing words (for example holiday destinations) – again, the transmitter should picture the place in their mind. Also try guests' places of birth or unusual middle names if they don't know each other well. You could even try employing well-known songs by picturing the title as a scene.

If you have enjoyed this game you may also like to try:

Can You Read My Mind? (see page 27)

Guess My Aura (see page 46)

Psychic Pass the Parcel (see page 67)

SONG OF SOLOMON LOVE GAME

What is it?
A light-hearted medieval game for discovering the identity of a future lover.

Number of players
Two to ten.

Event
For singles' nights, all-girls' evenings, Christmas and New Year parties (New Year's Eve is when it was traditionally played). To be played when the lights are low and people are settling down towards the end of the evening – in earlier times the game was started at midnight.

ABOUT THE GAME

This game works on the premise that we all have more than one person who could make us happy in love. Those in relationships may find that their partner's initials appear during the course of the game, or someone else's – perhaps those of a secret admirer who can remain as an ego boost and aphrodisiac for their present relationship.

This game uses the principle of dowsing (employing the movement of a pendulum, or wooden or metal rods, to find something hidden). It also involves reciting a very old love spell. The game has its origins in folk magic, which was incorporated into Christianity in around the sixth century AD – hence the use of a Bible here. The game was still regularly played by young unmarried women until the 1950s.

EQUIPMENT

1. Twenty-six cards or pieces of small square paper on which you have written the alphabet

If you laminate these or make them with stiff card you can keep them for future games.

2. Large door key

3. Long, thin red ribbon or cord from which to suspend the key

4. Small Bible
The King James version is best.

Game in a hurry
A crystal pendulum on a chain, a pendant or a plumb bob from the local DIY store can be substituted for the key and ribbon. You can buy Lexicon alphabet cards or a child's set of alphabet-learning cards instead of making your own.

HOW TO PLAY

* You (the hostess) should dim the lights, shuffle the alphabet cards and set out the letters face up in a clockwise circle on the floor, in the order of dealing. The circle of cards should be large enough for each individual to walk around inside it, in turn.

* Leave space between the first and last letters for the individual players to enter and leave the circle.

* Put the key and the ribbon apart in the centre of the circle.

* Invite everyone to sit or kneel around the outside of the circle.

* Holding the Bible open at the Songs of Solomon Chapter 8, verses 6 and 7, explain the rules and purpose of the game and then recite the words:

6: Set me as a seal upon thine heart, as a seal upon thine arm: for love is strong as death; jealousy is cruel as the grave: the coals thereof are coals of fire, which hath a most vehement flame.

7: Many waters cannot quench love, neither can the floods drown it: if a man would give all the substance of his house for love, it would utterly be contemned.

✴ Afterwards set the Bible on the floor in the centre of the circle and place the key and ribbon (still apart) between the open pages.

✴ The first person who volunteers enters the circle, kneels and ties the ribbon on to the key (only the first person does this).

✴ She then repeats the words from the Song of Solomon and puts the open Bible back on the floor in the centre.

✴ Holding the ribbon with the wedding ring finger, she walks clockwise around the inside of the circle of letters, allowing the key to swing over each of the letters, and moving from one to the other very slowly.

✴ She continues walking (making more than one circle if necessary) until the key remains still over one of the letters. This letter is the first initial of the true love or unknown admirer's first name.

✴ Leaving the chosen letter in place, she continues around the circle of letters, again allowing the key to swing.

✴ When the player comes to another letter over which the key remains still, that is the initial of the love's surname.

✳ The game continues until everyone who wishes to do so has identified their love's initials.

THE RESULTS

Afterwards the rest of the group can help each other to guess the names of the lovers, however unlikely. Since love and dislike are so close, a prospective lover may be a person the player heartily dislikes or considers arrogant.

   You can set the tone for guessing the names according to the nature of the party and the sensitivities of those present. PC could be anything from Prince Charles to Peregrine Cuthbertson.

TIP If players let their minds go blank as they walk around the circle of letters, an image of a possible love or secret admirer (they may already know them) should appear in their minds.

FOLLOW-UP ACTIVITIES

If not many people are playing, each person can, after guessing the initials, walk around the circle again, asking a question about the future lover, this time selecting three letters with the key and ribbon. In this case the initials and the questions are discussed straight after each person's turn rather than after waiting until everyone has had a turn, and again everyone helps with suggestions. For example, the player might ask where the prospective lover lives or where they will meet. The answering letters of 'B T H' could suggest the 'city of Bath' or 'the swimming baths', or they may indicate that he may turn up while the questioner is having a bath.

The idea is for the whole group of players to be as ingenious as possible, and they can also suggest further questions to ask if there is time, for example: 'What is his job?' 'W T R' might give 'writer', 'waiter' or any number of possibilities, including 'waster'. Or, what does he like doing best? 'D R G' might suggest 'drinking home-brewed beer', 'driving fast cars', 'dredging canals for old supermarket trolleys', 'dragging (partners by the hair?)', and so on.

If you have enjoyed this game you may also like to try:
Astro Twins (see page 12)
Guess My Dark Secret (see page 81)
Halloween Party Games (see pages 123–143)

GUESS MY AURA

What is it?
An easy, active aura-reading game that combines psychic skill with a traditional party game.

Number of players
Six to fifteen.

Event
Good bonding exercise at work parties or training seminars. Also great for mixed and single-sex informal day and evening events, held either indoors or outdoors, and for singles' evenings and gatherings involving relative strangers as well as friends.

ABOUT THE GAME

Every person is surrounded by a constantly moving and changing energy field. It can be seen or sensed brightly around the whole body, and at parties, where people tend to be relaxed and animated, it is particularly visible around the head. The fact that people are relatively at ease at social gatherings makes parties ideal venues for seeing auras.

The field is seen or sensed psychically as rainbow colours, one of which usually predominates to indicate the personality or mood of the individual. We can all see and feel auras but generally doubt this ability. However, a great deal of information can be obtained about a person's personality, current mood and potential from becoming aware of their personal energy field. Touch is the best way to tune in to someone's energy field, although you actually make little physical contact with the body.

The aura field extends about an arm span all around the body and can be felt as a slightly sticky membrane. It feels lightest the further away from the body you get. In the game the person feeling the aura of a chosen subject is blindfolded, so they operate entirely on touch, using the sensitive fingertips linked to the palm energy centres, or chakras, that are also used in the psychometry game, You Really Were an Awful Child (see page 57). Since the subject is chosen at random and does not speak, the guesser is free to talk and speculate without worrying about fitting the intuitive fingertip information with expectations about the subject.

EQUIPMENT

1. Blindfold

2. Lively compilation music on tape or CD, and a player

HOW TO PLAY

❋ Before you begin, demonstrate the aura by asking participants to stand with their two palms facing inwards about 10 cm apart (holding the arms slightly away from the body with elbows bent). Tell them to move their palms in and out very slowly so that the palms almost touch. Gradually, a sticky sensation will be felt, the hands will become heavy and some people may detect a glow around the edges of the fingers.

❋ When the game begins everyone stands in the centre of the room and a volunteer is chosen and blindfolded.

❋ The other players dance or gyrate around the volunteer to the music.

❋ When the music is stopped (after about a minute and a half), the dancers stand still and the volunteer reaches out until they touch one of the unmoving figures.

❋ Everyone else backs away and the selected subject remains still and silent.

❋ The volunteer moves outwards with their hands to what they assess is an arm span on either side of the subject. With palms vertical and fingertips outstretched and slightly curved, they then weave in and out of the aura space of the subject. They should pay special attention to the area around the head and shoulders, where the aura is strongest. Once they touch the physical body, they must move their hands away again and keep them moving continuously.

* The volunteer should talk out loud about what they sense the person is like from what they feel in the aura – they should talk about their lifestyle, likes and dislikes and if they sense any colours around the person. Touch is just as effective as sight for spotting aura colours.

* After two minutes, you should stop the game. The subject should return to the group before the blindfold is taken off the volunteer.

* Another volunteer is then blindfolded and the game continues.

THE RESULTS

Sitting down with a drink, the victims can identify themselves and a general discussion can take place about the results. Volunteers may have picked up on one or more colours and here is a guide to what type of personality they represent:

Red Fiery and passionate
Orange Very self-confident and creative
Yellow Logical and clever
Green Sympathetic and loving

Blue Idealistic and a natural leader
Purple Dreamy and psychic
Brown Practical and cautious
Black A dark horse with masses of secrets
Pink Patient and an animal lover
Grey Versatile and a natural peacemaker
Neon colours A real extrovert and a flirt

TIPS Remember that everyone can sense and see auras.

The key to a blindfolded volunteer's success is to keep their hands weaving in and out, talking continuously without pausing to consider whether they are right or to gauge a reaction.

FOLLOW-UP ACTIVITIES

Sit in a circle. The first person chosen turns to the person on the left, stares hard at them and closes their eyes, blinks and says the first colour they see around the subject or that comes into their head, for example 'Green'. You should keep this going around the circle as fast as possible. The colour will usually coincide with any information picked up through touch earlier. Again, afterwards everyone can join in and reveal the colours they saw around different people.

If you have enjoyed this game you may also like to try:
Past Life Game (see page 20)
You Really Were an Awful Child (see page 57)
Psychic Pass the Parcel (see page 67)

NOW YOU SEE IT

What is it?
A quiet, relaxed psychic imagery game, based on a fascinating but little known psychic skill identified in adults as well as children.

Number of players
Minimum of six.

Event
Any intergenerational gathering or any age group – the game can be played on occasions such as Christmas, birthdays or anniversaries, or after supper parties; good for winding down at the end of an evening.

ABOUT THE GAME

Eidetic imagery was first researched by psychologists in relation to children. One explanation for night terrors in children was that they might be 'eidetic images', pictures which are so vivid in a child's mind that they project them into their surroundings like a cinema projector throws images onto a screen.

Experiments have been carried out in which a child is shown a picture, which is then removed. According to the tests, between 30 and 90 per cent of children tested could point out numerous details as though the absent picture was still there.

Adults also have this power, although they are rarely aware of it and only a few have a true photographic memory for recalling pages of words or numbers. This game calls upon the use of this power.

EQUIPMENT

1. Pale, blank wall
You will need to insert a nail or hook if you are using posters or prints.

2. Three or four pictures
These need to have identifiable details that could not be deduced logically. Abstract paintings won't do. Choose lesser known works of famous painters so they are less likely to be familiar. Works by Turner, John Waterhouse, Holman Hunt, Constable, Lowry, Van Gogh and Renoir are my favourites for the game.

You can use actual paintings as long as they are only thinly framed and without glass. Have a hanging cord attached to each picture so that you can put it up and remove it from the wall fast.

3. Projector and slides (alternative to hung pictures)
Use slides of, for example, townscapes, beaches with distinct groups of figures, well-ordered gardens, etc. Ensure each image fills at least a quarter of the wall area chosen.

4. Pads and pens
You will need these for each player to sketch details.

5. Visible clock with large second hand

Game in a hurry
Just play the game once with a painting that you usually have in a part of the house regular guests to your home will not have seen.

HOW TO PLAY

* Stand everyone in front of the blank wall and explain the rules. Each picture should be set in place or projected for just 45 seconds.

* Guests should stare as hard as possible at the image, but should not try to memorise the details.

✳ Remove the picture. The guests should continue to stare at the now blank wall for a further 60 seconds, as though the picture was still there, trying to see the different areas of it.

✳ After 60 seconds say, 'Now draw the picture.' Guests must scribble and use rough notes to recreate the details of the pictures on their pads, glancing at the blank wall as necessary to refix the imagery in their minds.

✳ After a minute tell the guests to stop, and put the image back on the wall.

✳ Those guests who correctly located seven or more features go into the next round of the game.

✳ Repeat the process with a new picture/projection and the second time eliminate anyone with less than ten features identified.

✳ If you have expert eidetic imagers present (for some reason those who work with money or are teachers are very good), you can use a third picture and this time eliminate anyone with less than 12 features identified.

✳ Repeat the process with the final picture/projection (if you have one) to see who identifies the most features.

✳ If no one identifies more than seven features the first time, everyone should try the second picture. If no one identifies more than ten features the second time, let all the remaining contestants try the third picture, and so on.

* You can end the game at any time after one picture has been viewed, depending on the mood/skill of the guests. If you get a really unobservant lot of guests, lower the targets after picture one.

THE RESULTS

The winner of the game will be the person who identified the most details in the final picture in the series. However, the overall eidetic champion will be the guest with the highest number of features identified in all the pictures shown (sometimes but not inevitably the same person).

TIPS Trying to memorise the pictures is counter-productive as this seems to block eidetic imagery.

The key to success is to keep staring at the wall whether or not the picture is there, rather than to try and see it in the mind's eye.

FOLLOW-UP ACTIVITIES

Use a series of postcards of detailed scenes of paintings or enlargements of holiday pictures in a similar way. Individual guests or small groups can set them one at a time on a table covered with a white cloth, stare down at the picture, remove it, stare at the white cloth and then record the images.

If you have enjoyed this game you may also like to try:
I Spy With My Clairvoyant Eye (see page 35)
Guess My Aura (see page 46)
Pass the Crystal Ball (see page 86)

YOU REALLY WERE
AN AWFUL CHILD

What is it?
A psychometry or psychic touching game using personal objects
from school days or childhood.

Number of players
Four to eight.

Event
This can be played at after-supper parties for new friends or
colleagues, at getting-to-know-you evenings for students or house-
mates, or after a small party to introduce prospective couples.

ABOUT THE GAME

Psychometry, or psychic touching, is the easiest psychic power to instantly access. Every object has an energy field or aura around it. This invisible energy field is made up of accumulated emotions and situations experienced by the owner of the item as they carried it with them or wore it over a period of time. These impressions become imprinted on the object. By touching the item, our hands (which have sensitive energy centres in the palms that extend to the fingertips) can tap into the object's stored information. If, for example, you hold an item from someone's childhood, you can pick up all kinds of information about the owner of the object when they were younger. This will include jokes they played at school, embarrassing moments and those best-forgotten crushes, all of which can be revealed in this game.

EQUIPMENT

Any personal item from school days

Anything from a school scarf or hat to a prefect's badge, an old pencil case, a small graffiti-covered exercise book, a photo, a Valentine's card or an old report card. Items should be as unusual or funny as possible. Don't forget to ask your guests to bring along an item when you invite them to the party.

HOW TO PLAY

* Everyone needs to sit in a circle. Items will be passed round the
  whole group, one at a time.

* Each person in the circle should close their eyes and hold the
  chosen item being passed around for a short time (usually about
  30 seconds) in order to focus their inner psychic senses. Using
  their fingertips as a guide, continuously running them over the
  object, they should start talking (without thinking what to say)
  about the childhood or school days of the owner of the object.
  They must talk about what they see in their minds, impressions
  they feel and any words that come to them, but should stop when
  they have no more information. When they finish they can open
  their eyes.

* The game starts with the item belonging to the person sitting on
  your (the host's) right. You can start the proceedings and when
  you have finished talking about the item you should hand the
  item to the person sitting on your left.

* That person holds the item with their eyes shut and then starts talking. When finished she hands the item to the next person on the left, until the object has been around the whole circle and is back with the owner.

* The owner of the item then comments on what has been said.

* Next you hand your own possession to the person on the left. The participants again come up with anecdotes until the item reaches you again. You then comment on the accuracy of the information.

* The person on your left then passes their memorabilia to the person on their left, who comments, and so on.

* Of course, guests will see each other's items before the game, but often they still reveal totally unexpected facets of their person- ality. For example, a prefect's badge might reveal how someone lost it due to being caught smoking behind the bike sheds.

* The game ends when everyone's item has been read.

THE RESULTS

A general discussion inevitably follows about school days and the memories triggered by the items. Usually some of the information is very accurate and other parts have picked up half a story – that can now be finished.

TIPS *You and the other participants should talk, talk, talk and keep talking – mention whatever comes into your head as you hold each object, including words, images and impressions. Don't stop to rationalise or second-guess as then your conscious mind (rubbish at psychic games) will take over.*

Let your fingertips not your eyes transmit the information – so keep touching and turning the object as you speak to maintain the link.

FOLLOW-UP ACTIVITIES

Have ready a family treasure or two: a cup from your great-grandmother's tea set, a ring that has been in the family for generations, a great-grandfather's pocket watch. Ask the group to hold the items one by one and say whatever comes into their minds about where they see the object being used and any impressions of its former owners. When everyone has finished passing the item around and talking, you can tell them the information that you know about it.

If people are really into psychometry after this, you can ask volunteers to hand round current items like watches and car keys and to ask questions about the owner's future. Such items also hold information about our potential, so this is another effective method of prediction.

If you enjoyed this game you may also like to try:
Psychic Pass the Parcel (see page 67)
I Spy with My Clairvoyant Eye (see page 35)
Now You See It (see page 51)

TRUTH OR DARE?

What is it?
A psychic version of this popular game where the pendulum gets to choose whether it's truth or dare. If it is truth, the pendulum can reveal if the person is lying and will match the dare with the victim.

Number of players
From two up to about fifteen people – the more the better.

Event
For family gatherings, hen and stag nights, and parties with close and new friends of similar age.

ABOUT THE GAME

This is a more exciting version of the well-known game because the players are relying on their unconscious minds, which cannot so easily lie. Nor can they set others up for a rotten dare – or fix it so they get to kiss who they fancy!

The pendulum is controlled by the unconscious muscular responses of the arm that in turn moves according to the promptings of the deeper parts of the mind. This makes it hard to cheat (it is estimated that about 70 per cent of people stray from the truth in a typical game and most get away with it).

EQUIPMENT

1. Large, clear crystal pendulum

2. List of 30 pre-written dares on identical squares of paper or card

Before you play the game, get together with another person who is attending the party and knows the approximate ages and background of the partygoers. Obviously you'd write different dares if playing with your mother and her cousins than you would at a hen night. You can be quite specific.

3. Empty dark glass bottle

A wine bottle is best.

HOW TO PLAY

❋ Everyone sits in a circle on the floor or on cushions. You, the hostess, hold the pendulum and demonstrate the truth/lie responses. You say something that everyone knows is true and the pendulum will spin clockwise. You then tell a blatant lie and the pendulum will spin anti-clockwise.

❋ Set the dares face down in the circle – they should be distributed evenly in the space (not in a pile).

❋ Also put the bottle in the centre of the circle.

❋ Before you start, demonstrate to the group how the pendulum chooses dares: hold the pendulum a few centimetres above each of the dares in turn and the pendulum will pull down over one with a vibrating movement as if tugged by gravity. Don't turn it over on this occasion unless someone volunteers to carry out the dare.

❋ Begin by spinning the bottle – the hostess does this first.

✳ As the bottle is spinning, pass the pendulum around fast clockwise from person to person, saying alternately, 'Truth/dare, truth/dare,' faster and faster, passing the pendulum faster until the bottle stops spinning.

✳ According to whether the person who the bottle points to says 'Truth' or 'Dare' that is the option they must offer to their chosen victim.

✳ They then choose the person they want to question from the group.

TRUTH OPTION
They ask the chosen person any question and hand them the pendulum. The victim answers the question, but must hold the pendulum still in front of them. If it spins clockwise that is fine – the truth has been revealed and the game continues; the victim is next to spin the bottle and passes the pendulum around as before.

DARE OPTION
If the pendulum says the victim is lying (it will spin anti-clockwise), then the questioner gets to choose the victim a dare by holding the pendulum over the face-down dares. The pendulum will pull down over the chosen dare. The questioner then reads the dare out loud, and the victim carries out the dare and then starts the game again by spinning the bottle.

Each time a dare is used it must be removed.

✳ The game ends when everyone has truth or dared (some people may get more than one turn), or when you run out of dares.

TIP *No one should try and fool the pendulum – they can't. In fact it's easy to see whether a person is deliberately trying to turn the pendulum clockwise, because the pendulum will usually respond by spinning the other way really fast.*

FOLLOW-UP ACTIVITIES

You can use the pendulum informally for making predictions for each other about the future as long as the questions can be answered with 'Yes' or 'No'.

If you all sit in a circle, one person asks the question and the person sitting to their right holds the pendulum to get the answer. You can continue around the circle as long as you like. The 'Yes' response is the same as the truth (clockwise spinning), the 'No' the same as the dare (anti-clockwise). If the pendulum doesn't move then it's saying that the questioner will have the choice.

If you enjoyed this game you may also like to try:
You Really Were an Awful Child (see page 57)
Guess My Dark Secret (see page 81)
What's My Future? (see page 91)

PSYCHIC PASS
THE PARCEL

What is it?

A psychic version of an old childhood favourite, pass the parcel.
Here the guests must guess clairvoyantly the contents of the box
inside the parcel.

Number of players

Minimum of six and any maximum.

Event

Ideal for any event, from house parties to barbecues, post-holiday
celebrations, teenage sleepovers or Christmas and birthday parties.
An excellent antidote game for world-weary sophisticates of any age.

ABOUT THE GAME

Antidote games like this are ideal at any point where boredom, antipathy between particular guests or after-meal malaise may lead to tension.

Remote viewing is another form of clairvoyance. This is a technique where a viewer can detect an unknown object, person or scene beyond the range of the physical eye. Some people can not only see, but also hear sounds or detect fragrances connected with the scene or object.

In the 1970s, intensive research was carried out into remote viewing abilities by Russell Targ and Harold Puthoff at Stanford Research Institute International in California in the United States. They concluded that remote viewing is a psychic power that many people experience spontaneously. Even subjects who had little previous psychic experience could quite easily be taught to 'see' and describe the contents of opaque containers.

EQUIPMENT

1. Mystery item
You can choose any item and it can be as unusual as you like, but it must be small enough to fit inside the box.

2. Bubble wrap

3. Small box to hold mystery item

4. Wrapping paper

You will need about 12 layers of wrapping paper per item (or more if you have lots of players).

5. Suitable music

You may want to create a mix tape with magic theme songs such as 'I Put a Spell on You'.

Game in a hurry

Place the object in a sealed decorative box, a series of nested cardboard boxes or a number of gift bags decreasing in size.

HOW TO PLAY

❋ Before the guests arrive, you as the hostess should wrap the mystery item in bubble wrap before putting it in the box (to prevent it from rattling).

❋ The box should be sealed and wrapped in about 12 layers of wrapping paper. Each layer should be sealed.

❋ When the guests arrive, ask them to sit in a tight circle and pass the parcel twice around the circle (clockwise) as fast as possible. As each person holds the parcel they should say, 'What's in the box?' as fast as they can before passing it on to the person on their left.

※ When the box has been around the circle twice, offer a general clue about the mystery object. This can be as cryptic and ingenious as you wish, for example, 'Older than you, older than me, dinner's at eight, better be late' (for prehistoric shark's tooth).

※ Then start the music, and the guests should pass the box around (as fast as possible) to the person on their left.

※ When you stop the music (after a minute and a half maximum), the person holding the box says, 'What's in the box?' and must then immediately make a guess about the box's contents.

※ If they are right, you should say so, and the correct guesser wins the game.

※ If they are wrong, they should undo a layer of the paper from around the box as fast as possible and then continue to pass it around when the music starts again.

※ If no one guesses by the time there is just the box, the box should be passed slowly around the entire group without music. Each guest puts their hands on the box and imagines a tunnel of light going down into the box like through a peephole. This is when the guests make their final guesses.

※ No indication is given whether or not these final guesses are correct, but the box is opened and the contents finally revealed.

THE RESULTS

You could have another prepared box to hand in case someone guesses the contents of the box very early on in the game. Alternatively, if no one guesses correctly, the box is opened. A number of guests may have been quite close in their guesses and everyone can discuss this.

TIPS Tell guests that they should pass the box around as fast as possible and to imagine that there is a hole in the wrapping and they can glimpse through it at the contents.

Tell them to picture the contents only as they hold the box and not to think about it as it passes around other people. The speed of the game should prevent this type of rationalisation.

FOLLOW-UP ACTIVITIES

You could also try this game with guests' handbags, a child's old lunch box or a backpack. Ask each guest in turn to psychically guess what items are contained in the bag without opening it – and give them 45 seconds to do this. Don't give any clues or reveal anything. Once everyone has had their go you can tip the contents out on the floor. Some items will be predictable, but judging by the contents of my handbag and those of my middle son Jack's Spanish backpack, many won't be.

If you have enjoyed this game you may also like to try:

Guess My Aura (see page 46)

You Really Were an Awful Child (see page 57)

Psychic Treasure Hunt (see page 73)

PSYCHIC TREASURE HUNT

What is it?
An outdoor dowsing or psychic hunting game to find hidden treasure.

Number of players
As many as you want.

Event
Garden parties, picnics, barbecues and any outdoor party. Children love this game. It is also brilliant as an Easter egg hunt. After all, in pre-Christian times, Easter eggs were painted in honour of Ostara, the Norse Goddess of Spring, and Oestre, the Anglo-Saxon goddess. The hare, our Easter rabbit, was her magic animal.

ABOUT THE GAME

Dowsing has been practised for thousands of years in ancient China and western Europe, and among the Native Americans and Australian Aboriginals – all hoping to find either hidden water or oil.

It relies on psychokinesis, whereby our automatic psychic radar picks up the location of a hidden object or objects. It can do this because everything has an aura or energy field round it and your unconscious mind tunes in to this physically invisible energy field even if the object is out of sight. The part we don't understand is why the rods seem also to respond independently to the stimulus. The hand and rod unconsciously move together to reveal the location of what is concealed.

Anyone can dowse and children are especially good at it because their conscious minds don't block the intuitive process by trying to work out the possible locations logically. Men also seem to be naturals at this external form of psychic power.

EQUIPMENT

1. Markers
You can use anything from stones to flags to mark out the perimeter of the area in which the game is being played.

2. Pre-hidden treasures of your choice
You can use anything you like, from miniature spirit bottles for adults to chocolates, coins, chocolate money, small, fluffy toys or

Easter eggs. Wrap the gifts in waterproof bags if it is damp. You will probably want to provide at least two or three treasures per person playing.

3. Pad and pen
You will need these to make a rough plan showing where the prizes are hidden.

4. Pair of identical L-rods for each player
If you only have a few guests playing you can use ready-made copper dowsing rods bought by mail order, on the Internet or from a New Age store. They are well worth having in your psychic games treasure chest as you will play this game again and again by popular request.

   If you do want to make your own dowsing rods you can use thin copper wire, thin ordinary pliant wire or coat hangers, and make them as follows. The wires used must be no more than 1 cm in diameter.

To use wire:

* For each rod you will need a 50 to 70 cm piece of wire. You can ask a DIY store to cut the wire for you, or do this yourself with a pair of wire cutters.

* Each of the pairs of rods is made from one piece of metal wire that must be bent. It should consist of a vertical section that is 15 to 25 cm long, which is held in the hand, and a horizontal section that is 30 to 45 cm long, which is at right angles to the handle.

* Make sure that the angle is 90 degrees between the handle and the main part of the rod.

* Each pair of rods should be the same size with identical handle lengths.

To use coat hangers:

* You will need two coat hangers for each pair of rods.

* Cut the coat hanger wire next to the hook and at one corner of the hanger.

* Straighten out the wire and make an L shape (as described above).

* For safety reasons, bend over each of the ends of the wire so that they are not too sharp. You can use biro tops as sleeves to shield the sharp wire ends.

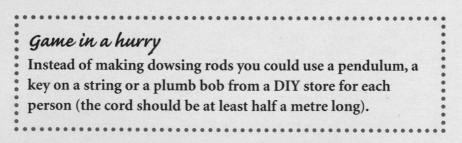

Game in a hurry

Instead of making dowsing rods you could use a pendulum, a key on a string or a plumb bob from a DIY store for each person (the cord should be at least half a metre long).

HOW TO PLAY

* You need to choose a relatively restricted area in which to play this game so no one is out of your range of vision – a large garden, an area of woodland or a park is ideal and you may want to use markers to show the perimeter.

* Make a rough plan of the area in which the game is being played.

* Before the guests arrive you will need to hide the treasures. You will probably need to provide about two or three treasures for each player (or more if you are using small objects like coins, chocolates or chocolate money).

* Hide the treasures at ground level or up to adult knee height.

* Make a note on your plan of where each object is concealed. Then if anyone is struggling you can guide them.

* Before the game begins, show everyone a sample of what has been hidden. This way they can visualise it in their minds while they are searching. This is essential for establishing the psychic link. You should also demonstrate how dowsing works with an object you have pre-hidden but know the location of (to save time and get the game going fast).

* Tell the players to hold the rods motionless before beginning, and to in ask their minds for the rods to find the targets.

* The rods are held horizontal to the ground and parallel to each

other so that the horizontal sections are level and pointing directly ahead as the dowser walks.

* Players should hold the handles (the short ends) of each rod quite loosely, so that the ends are in their closed vertical palms. They can place their thumbs on top of the clenched palm if this feels comfortable. They should hold the rods slightly away from the body, with the horizontals just above waist height and pointing straight ahead. The hands should be about shoulder width apart.

* If the direction of the treasure is not straight ahead the rods will swivel to point the correct direction and then remain straight as long as the path is correct. They will at any point spontaneously swivel or veer to the left or right if a player holding them needs to change direction, and will point ahead to show the new path to follow.

* The rods may vibrate the closer a player gets to a target, and when they are near a hidden item it may be harder to hold them straight. The rods may dip down if the object is hidden on the ground in, for example, a clump of flowers. They should be allowed to move as they want, and may get lower and closer to each other the closer a player gets to a target.

* When the rods identify a target, in this case a hidden object, they will spontaneously cross over each other above the spot. If the object is not immediately visible the player will need to look more closely to find it.

* If a pendulum (rather than rods) is being used, this will turn slowly in all directions and will start to swing clockwise when the correct direction has been chosen. It will continue to do this until the player starts to go in the wrong direction, when the pendulum will turn anti-clockwise. The player must again stop, turn slowly and try different directions until the clockwise motion returns. The closer to the target the player is, the more the pendulum will vibrate. This will be experienced as a tingling in the fingers and an ever-stronger clockwise swing, which will become intense over the target. At this stage the pendulum may, like the rods, pull down over the spot.

* Each time a player gets a prize they should hold it up and get everyone's attention.

* The game continues until you sense that the interest is waning or when everyone has found at least one item.

TIPS The key is to relax. If the players think of a gunslinger with his two pistols drawn they'll have the position for holding the rods right.

If it is windy they can lower the rods slightly from the straight-ahead horizontal position to offer more stability.

They should keep picturing the object in their heads and let the rods lead.

FOLLOW-UP ACTIVITIES

Guests can try to find underground water streams or water pipes using the same technique – or indeed gas pipes and electricity cables. As long as the player specifies the target in advance the L-rods will follow the chosen course. You can look at a few old plans in advance to find out where water etc., is so that you can tell guests if they have correctly located the target. If you have a subterranean well (a significant number of old properties do) ask guests to locate this.

If you have enjoyed this game you might also like to try:
Guess My Aura (see page 46)
Truth or Dare? (see page 62)
Psychic Pass the Parcel (see page 67)

GUESS MY DARK SECRET

What is it?
A group ice-breaking automatic writing circle game, based on our natural psychic ability to access information about others on a deep unconscious level.

Number of players
Six to twelve.

Event
An after-supper game at a singles' or mixed-sex dating evening or informal party, where people do not know each other very well; also hen nights and girls' nights in.

ABOUT THE GAME

Automatic writing was originally associated with spirit communication, but has in more recent and enlightened times been found to be an effective method of tapping into information not accessible on a conscious level.

By working as a group to tune into an individual's thoughts (with their consent) we can uncover not only the immediate information being recalled by the subject, but also all kinds of vivid details about their secrets. This information is contained within the subject's energy field, or aura, and is activated by remembering it. Secrets are excellent material for automatic writing because even those that occurred a few years ago are still endowed with strong feelings, a powerful transmitter of psychic information.

The hand controls the pen, and the words that are written by the players about their secrets come directly from a level not accessible consciously. The idea is to cut out the logical part of the brain that might try to deduce or second-guess the secret and would most likely fail. Automatic writing is another example of psychokinesis, the power of the mind to direct the hand, as in the Truth or Dare? pendulum game (see page 67).

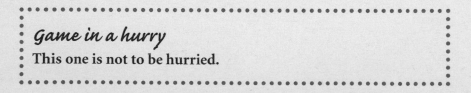

Game in a hurry
This one is not to be hurried.

EQUIPMENT

1. Pen for each guest
Traditionally the ink should be green.

2. Supply of pads of unlined paper
You will need a sheet for each secret being considered. Traditionally the paper should be cream and it should be thick so that the writing won't show through.

3. Soft lighting
One or two shaded lamps or tea lights – just enough light to write by.

4. Soft, slow background music
I would suggest either a soft, slow classical piece or New Age dolphin or rainforest sounds set to music.

HOW TO PLAY

* Everyone sits in a circle around a table with their pens in front of them.

* The first volunteer takes a pad from the centre of the table and writes their secret on the first sheet of the pad, keeping it well hidden. It should be a secret from the past five years (still very accessible in the aura or energy field).

* The secret must be true (as spoof ones will not work) but can be

about any topic, from peeing on a cheating boyfriend's tooth-brush to pretending that your great-aunt had died when you had tickets for the women's finals at Wimbledon.

* The volunteer folds the sheet of paper containing their secret, writes Top Secret on it, and keeps it in front of them. They focus for about half a minute on the secret they have written, picturing it visually for easy transmission. They then say to the person next to them on the left, 'Can you guess my dark secret?'

* They hand the pad to the person on the left, who picks up their own pen and without thinking starts to write a few lines about the secret.

* When they have finished they turn the sheet over so there is a blank page on top, hand the pad to the person on the left, and say, 'Can you guess the dark secret?'

* The game continues until the pad returns to the person with the secret.

* The subject reads out all the pages in turn without comment and then unfolds their sheet with the secret on it, and says, 'This is my dark secret.' You will be surprised at how close some people get.

* Another volunteer can continue the game in the same way, using a fresh pad.

* The game ends when people are bored with it – with small numbers everyone will want a turn.

TIPS *When players are writing their own secret to be guessed, they should try to imagine the scene as vividly as possible. They should concentrate on their feelings at the time, but also on any colours, sounds or fragrances. These create a multi-sensory experience for others to pick up on.*

The volunteer should picture the secret each time someone new starts to write.

When players are trying to guess the secret, they should hold their pens in the hand they usually write with and totally relax. They may feel a slight buzzing in their fingers. This is normal as their unconscious mind takes the driving seat.

FOLLOW-UP ACTIVITIES

There will obviously be lots of discussion about results and guilty secrets in general. People can then ask individual questions out loud about the future, and anyone interested can in turn write answers automatically, which can then be combined.

If you have enjoyed this game you might also like to try:
Truth or Dare? (see page 62)
Psychic Pass the Parcel (see page 67)
I Spy with My Clairvoyant Eye (see page 35)

PASS THE CRYSTAL BALL

What is it?
A psychic circle game that draws on the players' memories and has a predictive element.

Number of players
Up to twenty.

Event
Good for relative strangers, family and friends alike, especially inter-generational parties such as those that take place at Christmas. Also great for after-conference parties, or for breaking the ice if people aren't relaxing at a party.

ABOUT THE GAME

Every home should have a crystal ball, however small. Set in the centre of your home it will attract health, good luck and happiness. In an area where you work or on your office desk, it will be a natural money attractor and promotion bringer. It is also a fabulous decoration, especially when light shines on it and makes rainbows.

Crystal-ball reading uses a technique called scrying, which means seeing images within a reflective surface. Scrying in shiny surfaces has been practised in every culture and time. Crystal-ball divination became popular in Europe in the fifteenth century, when it was believed that spirits or archangels would appear in the crystal sphere. One of the most famous scryers was Sir John Dee (1527–1608), who was astrologer to Queen Elizabeth I. His crystal provided forewarning of the Spanish Armada.

Anyone can see images in a crystal ball as long as one is used that has inclusions (cracks and patterns within). When you look inside, you seem to see a landscape.

This game is similar to children's games where everyone in a circle adds a word to a given basic sentence, such as: 'I went to the grocer and bought…' The players have to remember the words that have gone before their turn and then add a new word when it is their turn.

In this game, as the crystal ball is passed around the circle of guests, each guest says what they see in the ball and must also recite the previous list of images that other guests have seen.

EQUIPMENT

A quartz crystal ball with inclusions

Crystal spheres with inclusions are much cheaper than perfect ones.
You don't need a very large one.

Game in a hurry

You can cut down the time it takes to play by going around the circle just once. You can also scry without a crystal ball by dropping a small handful of dried cooking herbs (rosemary and chives are clearest) on the surface of water in a large crystal bowl. Each person swirls the water as they pass it around the circle and identifies an image made by the herbs. This is easy and great fun as an alternative party game (see page 215 for image meanings).

HOW TO PLAY

* If it is a sunny day you can play this game outdoors or near a window by directing the sunlight into the ball to help see the pictures within. If it is dark you will need lots of lit candles in the room.

* Sit everyone in a circle and hold the crystal ball in both hands, turning it to catch the light. Explain to your guests that they will

see pictures formed by the light and the cracks. Give examples, such as horses, people, archangels, mountains, birds, stars and butterflies.

✳ Let everyone have the chance to hold the crystal ball and identify pictures before you start the game.

✳ Players can say as much or as little about their image as they like (up to a sentence long – for example, 'I saw three stars falling through the sky.').

✳ Start the game by saying, 'I looked in the crystal ball and I saw…' and add your description of what you saw. So, for example, you might say, 'I looked in the crystal ball and I saw three stars falling through the sky.'

✳ Hand the crystal ball to the person on your left, who looks into the ball and says, 'I looked in the crystal ball and saw three stars falling through the sky,' and then adds the image that they see – for example 'a huge butterfly on a magnolia tree'.

✳ They then hand the crystal to the person on their left. This third person looks into the ball and says, 'I looked in the crystal ball and I saw three stars falling through the sky, a huge butterfly on a magnolia tree and…' and they add their own image to the growing list.

✳ The game continues around the circle.

THE RESULTS

A player is out of the game when they fail to remember the list. The last person remaining is declared the winner.

TIPS Crystal-ball reading is fun and players should be encouraged to be as creative and inventive as they like about what they see. I have known people see steam trains or toilet seats in a crystal ball.

It may be easier to look into the ball through half-closed eyes.

FOLLOW-UP ACTIVITIES

At the end of the game, the individual images can be interpreted using the list on page 215 of the most common images that are seen. Some are really obvious, for example birds mean travel or getting a promotion (rising high), but partygoers can be as creative as they like. We can all interpret images and the interpretations I have given are just guidelines. Everyone at the party can join in when it comes to explaining what an image means for the person who saw it.

If you enjoyed this game you may also like to try:
Guess My Aura (see page 46)
Now You See It (see page 51)
Psychic Treasure Hunt (see page 73)

WHAT'S MY FUTURE?

What is it?
A fortune-telling game based on rolling dice. Dice predictions are said to come true within nine days.

Number of players
Two to ten.

Event
For any party, whether the guests know each other or not. An easy, mixed-generation game, good for male-orientated gatherings and pub evenings and also for birthday and anniversary parties.

ABOUT THE GAME

This game uses traditional number interpretations from ancient Greece, the Far East and Victorian England that have been adapted for the modern world.

Dice magic became popular among travelling people, especially those in fairs and circuses from the Middle Ages onwards. It reached its height for fortune telling in Victorian times, when it was a common party game among all classes of people. The same set of dice was generally used for gambling and for magic. Dice of ivory, wood, metal and glass, marked with dots like modern-day dice, have been discovered among the relics of ancient Egypt, Greece and Rome. In Tibet as recently as the nineteenth century, dice were used for foretelling events and not for gambling. Even today, Tibetan Buddhist lamas cast the dice and interpret the oracle for devotees.

EQUIPMENT

1. Three dice
Each marked with the traditional one to six spots on the faces.

2. Small cup, glass or dice shaker (optional)
For shaking the dice.

HOW TO PLAY

✳ The players sit around a table.

✳ Each person shakes the three dice in their cupped hands (or cup, glass or dice shaker) five times and says, 'Dice, dice thus I shake, tell me shall I my fortune make?'

✳ They then cast the three dice on to the table and add together the numbers of the uppermost faces.

✳ You, the hostess, reads out the meaning of the throw from this book.

✳ The person hands the dice to the person on their left, and the process continues until everyone has cast the dice and received a prediction.

THE RESULTS

THREE DICE RESULTS

3   Good luck, an unexpected but welcome surprise or windfall. Watch out also for an unplanned pregnancy close to you.

4   Put a lock on your wallet – money will flow out faster than it comes in. Avoid the once-in-a-lifetime unrepeatable bargain, or you'll get more than you bargained for.

5   A mythical dark-haired stranger will come into your life (although he or she may be blonde, a redhead or bald). One thing's for sure, they'll bring a whole new meaning to the words fun, adventure and happiness.

6 Watch out that you don't lose something valuable through carelessness – it could even be your heart. Button your lip at family gatherings and keep smiling.

7 Avoid gossip and rumour. You could be the next subject of malice. Don't spill secrets – least of all your own.

8 Maybe you're sailing a bit close to the wind legally or morally – or would like to be. You will be very tempted whether by a flirtation or some quick cash. Resist.

9 Love and romance are in the air, whether you're in a relationship or on the lookout for Mr or Ms Perfect. If you are single then they're nearer than you think. Wedding bells in the family.

10 A good time for the family, especially for matters concerning children or older people; success or promotion at work, too.

11 Legal or official problems will be resolved soon in your favour. Good for small wins in competitions or gambles.

12 An important letter will arrive with the good news you were hoping for, but it will involve a quick decision. Rely on a good friend for advice on whether to accept or not.

13 Lucky for women. A time for men to listen to the womenfolk in their lives and stay close to home.

14 Be patient. If you go along with the present situation things will turn out your way.

15 I'm going to make you a star. Hidden creative talents will get a lucky break – whatever they are.

16   On the move – career, home or travel. Change is favoured, so get out there and move and shake.

17   Ask for whatever you want (or need), for this is the wish number, and a time when your requests will be favourably received.

18   Overseas connections are favoured, whether business, relatives visiting from overseas, unexpected money from across the water or a chance to go abroad for an unexpected trip; any planned journeys will go well.

TIPS Participants should ask a question in their minds before shaking the dice. The dice will usually answer it, or will foretell an event that will affect the event they were thinking of.

Don't forget – dice predictions are said to come true within nine weeks.

FOLLOW-UP ACTIVITIES

People will want to discuss the results. Four or even five dice can be cast for a second prediction. Just add all the numbers of the four or five uppermost faces together and read the prediction from the list below.

USING EXTRA DICE

19   You'll buy or be given something that will increase greatly in value. A good time for bargain hunting or speculation.

20   Watch out for overly critical people at work and anyone who tries to play the guilt-trip card.

21 Health matters are well aspected. A surge in energy and confidence – and masses of compliments.

22 The ultimate power number; you're definitely a very high flyer indeed. Get everyone to buy you a drink now before you get rich and famous.

23 Unexpected friends or family visitors will stay longer than expected. If you were planning a twosome watch out for someone else wanting to come along (or get in on the act).

24 Invest or spend wisely and you will double your money.

25 You're in love, or if unattached a secret admirer will be revealed.

26 You'll find something you thought you'd lost for ever, or someone from the past will return.

27 You'll get a hunch about a new opportunity or job; follow it even if others tell you it's a mistake.

28 Time for homes and gardens – or maybe finding the ideal nest for yourself (and a possible other). DIY or home-making are well aspected (even if normally out of character).

29 Don't spend too much time on details. Now is the time when creative ventures will succeed, but only if you launch them boldly and don't panic at the last minute.

30 Births, engagements, celebrations and parties, or an addition to the family are in the air – maybe through remarriage.

If you enjoyed this game you may also like to try:

I Spy with My Clairvoyant Eye (see page 35)
Domino Speculation Power Game (see page 98)
Who Will Be a Millionaire First? (see page 107)

DOMINO SPECULATION POWER GAME

What is it?
A predictive speculation game using dominoes. The winner is deemed to be the entrepreneur of the evening and millionaire of tomorrow.

Number of players
Four to twelve.

Event
For a late night with friends or acquaintances, for outdoor events that turn into indoor parties because of bad weather and for impromptu evenings that become a party.

ABOUT THE GAME

Dominoes originated in China in around the sixth century AD. They became very popular in the Middle East, probably when they were carried via the trade routes to China and Japan. They were not introduced into Europe until the middle of the eighteenth century. Gradually they took their place as a form of family divination, along with tea-cup reading and dice casting.

As well as an overall winner of this game, there is the 'dark horse of the party', who will surprise everyone one day by making a sudden huge pile of money or becoming president of an obscure republic. The dark horse is the person who deals most increasing value or 'power' dominoes.

Dominoes consists of two halves with different numbers of spots on each half. They can be placed either way around in the course of a game. Whether an individual domino is a 'power' domino depends on its value increasing when read left to right once it has been set down correctly to fit into the game. So a two followed by a three is a power domino but a three followed by a two is not.

The first domino chosen at random at the beginning of the game has a predictive message for the person who selects it. This 'key for fame and fortune' reveals future opportunities and pitfalls at work or in speculation.

EQUIPMENT

1. One or two identical sets of dominoes
You can use three sets if you have more than eight players or if you want a lengthy game.

2. Pen and paper for each person playing

This is so each player can write down the first domino they set down as it has a fortune-telling meaning. They can also calculate the number of power dominoes they set down.

3. Prizes (optional)

You may want a prize such as chocolate money or a bottle of bubbly for the entrepreneur of the evening and a pair of dark glasses for the dark horse.

Game in a hurry
Don't take note of the power dominoes and don't worry about choosing a dark horse.

HOW TO PLAY

* If more than four players are in the game, set down two sets of dominoes (58 in all) face down in the centre of the table.

* Mix the dominoes, still face down, and ask each player to select four from the central dominoes.

* Each player arranges the dominoes as a wall in front of them so the other players can't see the values.

* The first domino selected should be noted by each player as this

is their predictive one, but its identity must not be revealed until the end of the game.

* The person with double six starts the game, setting the domino flat on the table, near the centre, face uppermost.

* If no one has the double six, the players in turn select an additional domino from the centre to add to their wall, going around from left to right through the players, until the double six appears. As soon as it is picked it can start the game.

* If two players have the double six, they have to run around the table three times and the first to set it gets to lead. (This may become a threesome if you are using three sets.)

* Every time a player needs to pick up a domino from the centre to add to their set, they say, 'Knock on wood, knock on tree, lucky for some, lucky for me.'

* A domino can only be set down to add to the central row if it contains a spot that matches one end of the original domino and thereafter each end of the growing row.

* The person to the immediate left of the holder of the double-six sets the first domino so that one end matches one of the sixes, for example blank and six or one and six. If they don't have a domino with a six and so can't go, they pick up another domino from the centre.

* Each time a domino is set down on either of the ends of the row

the player should note if it has an increasing or decreasing value from left to right.

* A player can continue adding dominoes to the central row until they can go no further.

* Then it is the turn of the person on their left. If they can't add a domino to the line they pick up a domino from the central face-down group, and then it is the next person's turn. Putting down the domino you pick up straight away only applies to the first double six.

* Strategically, when a player has an option of adding to either end of the row it is better to put down a domino that increases in value from the left when it is set down. Therefore, if you had a four at both ends of the row and wanted to put down your three-four domino, add it to the four at the left end of the row so that it becomes a power domino because of its position.

* The winner is the person who puts all his dominoes down first and he is the entrepreneur of the evening.

* The game finishes at this point.

THE RESULTS

Each player adds up the number of power or increasing dominoes. The person with the most increasing dominoes is dark horse of the evening. In the event of a tie, have your contestants make domino towers; the highest not to crash is the dark horse.

Then the players can reveal their fame and fortune domino number and you can tell them their fate, based on the list of interpretations given below:

Double blank Not a great start for would-be speculators, but then someone's got to make the coffee.

One blank Fortune lies out on the road, not at a desk, so get out there and make your fortune.

Double one Take a chance on an unlikely prospect or a back runner – you'll make a swift and profitable return.

One-two Economise (or get a loan), for expenditure will soar and extra income will only follow slowly.

One-three Jackpot – you find the missing link or make contact with the person you've been trying to talk to for ages, and they say yes.

One-four Personal financial gains through an original idea or a creative venture; don't forget to patent it.

One-five A love affair furthers your career, if you keep your head and your promises.

One-six Someone causing trouble at work or for your business will soon be on their way.

Blank-two A delay in your plans may cause temporary cash-flow problems; stall and hang on in there until Lady Luck smiles again.

Double two A double success in your bid for the top; you may get a new partner in crime or an unexpected ally.

Two-three You will get reliable insider information; follow it and you'll make a profit.

Two-four A totally unpredicted increase in good fortune – maybe a bonus or investment or input you had forgotten about.

Two-five Overseas connections or outlets will prove a distinct advantage; a good time for relocation.

Two-six A gift or an offer may not seem like a golden opportunity, but will open a long-term path to success.

Blank-three Scandals, jealousy, backbiting and secret empire building – make sure you keep your nose clean for the inevitable fallout.

Double three Now is the time to ask for promotion, more money or recognition, as a reward for your efforts is long overdue.

Three-four A face from the past will re-enter your work world, rekindling old rivalries or maybe old love interests. A good time to consolidate any business deals and to put temporary arrangements on a more secure footing.

Three-five Check your work thoroughly and don't take short cuts; it's not a time to make a mistake, as all eyes are on you.

Three-six Socialising and networking will pay dividends and maybe open doors to members'-only benefits.

Blank-four An angry email, letter or phone call needs careful handling as you may need the contact later; don't reveal sources.

Double four Guard your tongue and more radical opinions at work celebrations, leaving parties or after-seminar or lecture gatherings (walls have ears).

Four-five A speculation or risk turns out well, but take the winnings and don't test your luck again straight away.

Four-six Legal and official matters raise their heads; keep your head down and don't be too creative with your accounting or liberal with the truth.

Blank-five Wise counsel from an older person whom maybe you'd dismissed in the past; or even that mythical inheritance from a distant relative.

Double-five A move would be advantageous; check out the opposition and keep your eyes open – your rise could be meteoric.

Five-six Family or love affairs may temporarily distract you from your job; or an office flirtation gets out of hand.

Blank-six A new friend or colleague may be using your ideas or taking the credit to further their own career. Get a new password and watch your back.

Double six The power domino. Go for what you want – you can't fail.

TIP Traditionally Monday and Friday are not considered propitious for dominoes. One way to avoid any unfortunate results if the party falls on these days is for each guest to turn one garment inside out.

FOLLOW-UP ACTIVITIES

Mix all the dominoes, then place them face down and mix again. Guests can ask a specific question out loud and choose a domino to answer it.

If you enjoyed this game you may also like to try:
The Image Game (see page 3)
What's My Future? (see page 91)
Who Will Be a Millionaire First? (see page 107)

WHO WILL BE A MILLIONAIRE FIRST?

What is it?

A playing-card prediction game to see who can accumulate the most wealth during the course of the game – and also to make long-term predictions about money making.

Number of players

Five to twenty.

Event

Good for pub evenings, club events, leaving parties, work events, student parties and potentially boring family get-togethers.

ABOUT THE GAME

Playing cards have always been used for the dual purpose of games and prediction. They were probably invented in China in around the tenth century. European playing cards as we know them today originated in Egypt in around 1400. Four hundred years later Napoleon planned and is said to have won several battles and successfully wooed the Empress Josephine using the prophetic power of playing cards.

This game depends on strategy and memory, plus intuitive awareness and clairvoyant vision that instinctively draws a player to choose a particular face-down matching pair of cards. It is often this indefinable psychic quality that attracts money to some people (seemingly without effort) in everyday life because they are in the right place at the right time or know when to take a risk. Diamonds represents the wealth suit in this game.

Game in a hurry

Just focus on the predictive aspect. Each player in turn asks, 'Will I be a millionaire first?' and picks five cards from the shuffled face-down packs on the table. Count the total number value of the cards you picked; the potential millionaire is the one with the highest value cards. Any diamonds cards double in value, except for the jack, queen and king, which triple in value. The basic value of the ace is 1; jack is 11, queen 12 and king 13. You can then read what your hand is predicting about your financial future from the list of meanings in the follow-up activities (see page 129).

EQUIPMENT

1. Two or four identically backed sets of playing cards

You need a minimum of two packs for ten players.

2. Pen and paper for calculating values

HOW TO PLAY

* In the centre of the room, on a big table or the floor, shuffle the cards and spread them out face down in a circle.

* Players sit or kneel around the cards so they can reach them.

* Each player around the circle in turn flips over a card and tries to make a match with another face-down card. You match by number, for example two queens of any suit or of the same suit.

* When a player makes a match they should create their own personal pile of cards.

* The value of each card is the number shown on it and the basic

value of the ace is 1, jack 11, queen 12 and king 13. Any diamonds cards double in value, except for the jack, queen and king, which triple in value.

✳ A game is timed to last for ten minutes. Strategically, players therefore need quickly to make high-value card matches. They can do this by watching and memorising the positions of other players' cards from failed turns – and more importantly by using their instincts to guide their hands.

✳ The ultimate aim is to win the highest value cards in total, so any or all of the high diamonds in a pair are prized.

✳ On making a match the player is entitled to another turn and may continue having turns until their luck runs out. If they fail to make a match then it is the next player's turn.

✳ Guesses continue around the circle until time runs out. Players must pick up cards as fast as possible.

✳ The game ends after ten minutes or when all the cards have been won, whichever happens sooner.

✳ Don't forget to turn the cards back face down in the spread after a failed turn.

THE RESULTS

The players add up all the individual card values, ace (1) to 10, jack (11), queen (12), king (13). It is double for diamonds from ace to 10 and triple for the diamond picture cards. The winner has the highest number of points and is predicted to become rich first.

TIP If you are intuitive rather than a strategist, this game is for you since you will be able to respond much faster than someone who is memorising the places of the cards. When you turn over the first card visualise a beam of light linking it with another card and that will be your good match.

FOLLOW-UP ACTIVITIES

You can also use the cards you picked as pairs to predict how and when you will become rich.

Put your cards face down and shuffle or mix them around. Select one at random, to tell your financial fortune, using the meanings below. This can be a communal activity with one person reading the basic meanings from the book and everyone else adding their intuitive interpretations. Predictions can often occur quite swiftly, unless they refer to a long-term scheme.

Diamonds Accumulating wealth slowly but surely; long-term prosperity.
Hearts Wealth in terms of happiness and money earned through personally satisfying activities or through marriage.
Clubs Money through speculation and creative activities; a quick injection of money; the unexpected but advantageous.
Spades Expect setbacks and delays, although through adaptability

and endeavour excellent results can be obtained.

Aces New beginnings or unexpected opportunities for money making.

Twos Need to make choice or to juggle two commitments until one proves financially viable. Sometimes signify the possibility of a new business partner.

Threes Expansion of opportunity, promotion, small, sudden financial gains, rewards and payouts for earlier endeavours.

Fours Risks that may pay off, without which you won't progress to the big league of players. A good time for taking out loans or finding backers.

Fives Communication to encourage confidence in you and your products or skills; overseas contacts or travel bringing financial advantage – or talking your way out of trouble.

Sixes Quiet, stable period; time to consolidate assets or position, but beware of stagnation or complacency, also of hard luck stories from people who never pay you back.

Sevens Mysteries, secrets, illusion and maybe a con artist around you. Avoid offers too good to be true. They are. Maybe unexpected money through inheritance coming in.

Eights Make or break time. A big opportunity, but one that may involve disruption personally. Beware of over-spending on luxuries.

Nines Go it alone – don't lend money or share ideas; a personal venture will bear fruit if you don't hesitate or doubt your own talents.

Tens Solid financial backing or consolidation of your position – good for property deals; but also get rid of anything or anyone who is draining your resources.

Jacks A new acquaintance will have good ideas and a fresh approach, but watch your back. Alternatively the sudden revival of a money-making talent you'd given up on.

Queens Woman in authority or older woman will become significant in your personal as well as your work life and offer you unexpected support, advice and financial input.

Kings Older or powerful man will open a door for you; can also point to making a big gain or succeeding beyond your dreams financially; perhaps to do with a big promotion.

If you enjoyed this game you may also like to try:

What's My Future? (see page 91)
Domino Speculation Power Game (see page 98)
Now You See It (see page 51)

THE ARCHANGEL
WHEEL GAME

What is it?
A light-hearted board game in which the dark archangels seek to
overcome the forces of light and vice versa.

Number of players
Four to ten, but it must be an even number. Ten is the best number
because then all the archangels are in play at once.

Event
Any, from family parties to leaving events. The team aspect is also
good for getting to know strangers, acquaintances and business asso-
ciates better. Good for any age or sex.

EQUIPMENT

1. The archangel wheel

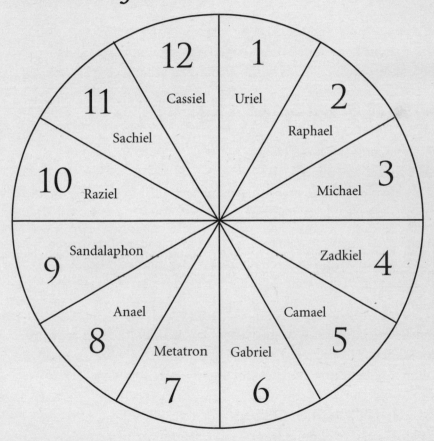

Scan or photocopy and enlarge the wheel, stick it on a card and laminate it so you can use it again. You can make it as large as you like.

2. Five small, flat black stones

Each should be painted or marked with permanent pen in silver or white with the initial of one of the dark archangels (see list below).

3. Five white stones

These should be painted or marked in permanent pen in gold or dark blue with the initials of the archangels of light (see list below).

4. One black and one white dice

5. The archangel list:

THE RULING ARCHANGELS
(These two don't take part in the game as such, but their segments are respectively heaven and hell.)

Michael (3) Supreme archangel of light and leader of the lesser archangels of light. His catch phrase is: 'Hail to thee, Michael of Radiance. So shall thy glorious light overcome darkness. Michael has dominion.'

Metatron (7) Supreme dark archangel and leader of the lesser archangels of darkness. His catch phrase is: 'Hail fearsome spirit of the night. So tremble all beneath your dreadful might. Metatron wins – again.'

THE LIGHT ARCHANGELS
(Michael rules over these.)
Raphael (2) The healing archangel of the dawn
Zadkiel (4) Archangel of truth and nature

116

Gabriel (6) Archangel of the moon
Anael (8) Archangel of love and gentleness
Sachiel(11) Archangel of charity and the harvest

THE DARK ARCHANGELS
(Metatron rules over these.)
SANDALAPHON (9) The tall twin and the archangel of cosmic fire
RAZIEL (10) Archangel of mysteries and the deep
CASSIEL (12) Archangel of silence and tears
URIEL (1) Archangel of fire and alchemy
CAMAEL (5) Leopard-clad archangel of war

Game in a hurry

Divide into two teams and have up to ten white and ten black unmarked stones in two pots. A dark and light archangel team member each throws a stone towards the wheel at the same time. The dark archangel throws a dark stone aiming to land on Metatron's hell. The light archangel is aiming for Michael's heaven.

If the stone lands in a friendly segment (that is, a light archangel segment for the light stone and vice versa), the stone is returned to the pot and may be thrown again in a subsequent turn. If a dark stone lands on Michael's heaven or a light stone on Metatron's hell it is removed from the game. If you hit an opponent's stone in mid air they lose their wings and are captured by the opposition.

Each team member takes turns to throw the stones. Throwing

is repeated until all dark or light player stones are in their own ruling archangel's heaven or hell or have been removed from the game. The first team with the most surviving archangels in Metatron's hell or Michael's heaven wins. Players can chant encouragement in the name of their ruling archangel.

HOW TO PLAY

* There are two teams who each control the dark or light forces. So if there are four players this means there are four archangels (two dark and two light), who will be in play at one time.

* The idea is to begin with all the chosen archangel stones placed initially in heaven or hell (the Michael or Metatron segment according to whether they are dark or light stones). Thus with ten players all ten stones are divided initially between Michael and Metatron's segments, whereas with four players four stones are divided between the segments.

* The aim of the game is for the individual archangels (represented by stones) to travel around the wheel eliminating opposing archangels, and fly around the cosmic wheel three times before returning safely home to heaven or hell.

* Each player has to begin the turn of their archangel by throwing a six using the black or white dice (according to whether they are a dark or light archangel) before they can begin moving. Once the

six is thrown they can have another throw of the single dice straight away, and move that many segments forwards (clockwise).

✳ If a light archangel lands on a dark archangel segment, the player has to name a really secret bad thing they have done to persuade the other team to let them rest there.

✳ However, if a dark archangel lands on a light archangel segment, the player must name a nauseatingly good deed they have performed to convince the light archangels that they are worthy of a resting place.

✳ If a light archangel lands on another light archangel segment, that is fine and they can rest there until the next throw; this is the same if a dark archangel lands on another dark archangel segment.

✳ If a light archangel lands on their own archangel segment, they can challenge any dark archangel anywhere on the wheel to combat and vice versa. If this happens they say, 'I challenge thee to summon thy powers that they may fall before my might.' This is optional.

✳ If they don't accept a challenge, the person who declines must miss a turn and the other person takes that turn straight away.

✳ If the challenge is offered and accepted, the light archangel must recite all six archangels of light and their titles three times (for example Gabriel of the moon, Zadkiel, archangel of truth and nature, and so on) in the order shown above, followed by their ruling archangel chant six times. At the same time the dark archangel must recite all dark archangel names and titles three times, followed by their warrior chant six times again as fast as possible.

* You will want to practise this in advance of the games as mistakes or being slower than the opposition result in the loser's stone being captured by the ruling opposing archangel and so being removed from the game. Fellow archangels can distract the opposition if wished.

* If a stone lands on its ruling archangel segment during the first two flights around the wheel, the player gets an extra turn.

* If a stone lands on the opposing ruling archangel segment at any time in the game, it remains captive and the player leaves the game.

* The challenge can also be offered by an archangel already on his own kind of segment if an opposing archangel lands on it while the first archangel is resident. If, however, the current resident is not on his own type of segment e.g. a dark archangel is resting on a light square, then the subsequent light archangel landing on that square can challenge that usurper. In both cases it is up to the true archangel to decide whether he wishes to challenge. If so the challenge must be accepted or a turn is lost.

* If two or more light archangels land on the same light archangel square (or vice versa with dark archangels), that is fine, although they must name themselves and recite their archangel chant together to bond.

* The game ends when all the archangels are back in their own domains.

THE RESULTS

The idea is to get all the archangels safely back to heaven or hell (Michael or Metatron's segment), having travelled the wheel unscathed three times. The game can be played so that there is a best of three (or more with fewer players). Suitable 'archangel and devil foods' can be offered as rewards.

TIPS Make sure everyone practises the archangel chant in advance of the game (you can appoint a coach for each team).

Play the game as fast as possible to keep up the momentum.

If small numbers are playing you can have more rounds in rapid succession, with players choosing different archangels if they wish to do so.

FOLLOW-UP ACTIVITIES

Confession time – initiate discussions as to the worst things the players ever did, maybe at school, at a first job or to a former partner, which never got found out.

If you have enjoyed this game you may also like to try:
You Really Were an Awful Child (see page 57)
Truth or Dare? (see page 62)
Guess My Dark Secret (see page 81)

HALLOWEEN
PARTY GAMES

DRUIDIC APPLE BOBBING

What is it?
This game is a traditional psychic Halloween love and fortune-telling game dating from Celtic times onwards. It will give a new slant to any Halloween party.

Number of players
Minimum of three.

Event
For adult or teenage Halloween gatherings large or small, mixed or single sex. Combine this section with games in Parts 2 and 3. Traditionally, all Halloween games should be completed by midnight. They can also be played at New Year's Eve parties, girls'

nights in and hen parties. You can play by firelight or near a Halloween bonfire.

ABOUT THE GAME

Halloween is traditionally the time for love games. This is because Halloween, or Samhain as it was called in Celtic times, was the beginning of the Celtic New Year and so a natural time for looking into the future, especially in matters of love.

Apple bobbing is an old Druid game. The Druids and Druidesses were the Celtic priesthood and organised the tribal or settlement celebrations. This game was one way in which lovers could divine a future marriage partner on the night when the dimensions between time opened (31 October).

A young person would pick up a floating apple with their teeth and then sleep with it beneath their pillow, which was supposed to enable them to dream of their future marriage partner (maybe someone they already knew or were dating). Apples were major fertility symbols associated with the Celtic Otherworld of magic and light.

The apples used in this game are marked with Ogham stave letters or symbols. These are named after the Celtic God Ogma, who ruled over wisdom and learning. Each sign represents a tree or magical plant, and in Celtic times one of the signs was engraved on each apple. By randomly choosing an apple, people might discover the personality of the future partner. I have listed the signs and their meanings in the results section and also given the modern initial each represents (see page 129).

EQUIPMENT

1. Minimum of 20 apples

These should be regular-sized apples with stalks and firm skins. If more than 20 people are playing you will need 40 apples.

2. Small, sharp knife (a paper or paring knife is ideal) to mark the symbols

Practise beforehand on a spare apple or two so that you will mark the surface without damaging the skin.

3. One bowl, the size and depth of a washing-up bowl

This should be half filled with water and must have space to fit 20 floating apples. Alternatively you can use a plastic baby bath. If you have 40 apples you can use two bowls or a children's inflated paddling pool. Traditionally a wooden barrel or water butt was used.

4. Small squeeze of lemon juice

This should be added to the water to prevent the apples from going brown before the game.

Game in a hurry

Put unmarked apples in the water and draw the Ogham symbols on squares of paper or round stones, using a permanent marker. Put them in a box or bag. When a guest picks an apple with their teeth, still holding the apple in their teeth they can choose a slip from the bag or box to identify their lover.

HOW TO PLAY

✳ First mark each set of 20 apples with one of the symbols (shown below) on each of the individual apples. Use the knife for this step. Score a dot at the bottom of each symbol as when the apple is held upside down the symbol may be confused with another one.

✳ Fill the bowl with water and add a squeeze of lemon.

✳ All the guests should try to pick up an apple from the surface of the water with their teeth and must keep trying till they do (to avoid a lonely old age!).

✳ Normal rules of courtesy and turn-taking should ideally apply, but Celtic games can degenerate a little.

THE RESULTS

Match the chosen symbol on your apple against the list below to discover the personality of your future love and their possible initial. The initials are taken from the old Celtic names for trees. Don't worry if you're pledged to a Constantine and get a D. The letter may occur not only as the initial of the first name but as a surname or middle name – or you may have a secret admirer. The personality traits are the best identifier.

Birch		An inventor or creator, someone always starting new things and often leaving them undone.	B
Rowan		Very protective of anyone vulnerable, incredibly psychic.	L
Alder		Solid in build, very practical, potentially very, very rich.	F
Willow		Sensitive and sympathetic, can be a hypochondriac.	S
Ash		Great traveller or commuter, healing hands.	N
Hawthorn		Can be prickly and critical, but very discreet.	H
Oak		Loyal, committed, reliable, can be dogmatic.	D

Holly		Changeable, can be pessimistic, but with great prospects for a top job.	T
Hazel		Sees both sides of every question, always even-tempered, can be indecisive.	C
Apple		Generous, sensual, very fertile (you have been warned).	Q & K
Vine		Fun loving, great partygoer, can be prone to occasional excesses.	M
Ivy		Faithful, home lover, can be possessive.	G
Fern/ bracken		Humorous or sarcastic, very talkative, a traveller.	J/Y, alternatively Ng in surname such as Mannering or Pickering
Blackthorn		Late developer romantically, serious but very observant.	V/Z, alternatively St as is Stuart or Str in Christian or surname e.g. Stratford

Elder	≢	Enigmatic, full of surprises, problems with timekeeping.	R
Pine	†	A political animal, focused but witty, hygiene enthusiast.	A
Gorse	‡	Initially hard to get to know, but very soft and gentle inside, a stayer.	O
Heather	≢	Passionate in every way, impulsive and poetic.	U
Aspen/ white poplar	≣	Quiet, nervous, but a natural peacemaker.	E
Yew	≣	Spiritual, endlessly patient, slow to change.	I

TIPS Players should think about the person who would make them happy, in their minds, as they are bobbing.

If they don't recognise their lover from people they know, they should allow an image to come into their minds of the person who would make them happy.

FOLLOW-UP ACTIVITIES

Take the apple home and sleep with it under your pillow. You will dream of your lover.

After apple bobbing you can have wedding races (to be played only by the unmarried or those definitely coming out of permanent relationships). Have ready a dish of raisins and lengths of thin string, about the length of a shoelace. Any two people should together thread six raisins along the string; then each takes an end of the string threaded with raisins and says together six times, getting faster and faster: 'The fruit is sweet, so is my love; first or last, at the altar meet. The spell is cast. Love do not tarry, but marry me soon.' The pair should then hold the string tight in their mouths – one at each end – first chewing on the string and then eating the raisins. Whoever eats most raisins will be the first to marry. If the pair eats an equal number of raisins, there will be a double wedding. Some people will want to keep trying with different guests until they win.

If you have enjoyed this game you may also like to try:
The other Halloween Party Games (see pages 133–144)
Song of Solomon Love Game (see page 40)
New Year Party Games (see pages 169–194)

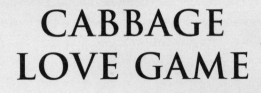

CABBAGE
LOVE GAME

What is it?
A Halloween love ritual described in a poem by the Scottish poet
Robert Burns, itself an adaptation of an earlier game from times
when root vegetables were the staple diet of the poor.

Number of players
Minimum of three.

Event
Halloween and New Year parties, hen nights; also outdoor events
and fundraisers; for any sex or age from teenagers upwards.

ABOUT THE GAME

Like all love divinatory games, this one is based on the belief that we all have someone or maybe more than one person who could make us happy. Older love games tend to be rooted in nature as this was believed to help us tune into our natural instincts to find the right mate.

   Players take turns to delve blindfolded into the tub and to pick out by touch and instinct the cabbage that holds clues to the identity of their future or indeed a present prospective lover.

EQUIPMENT

1. Two cabbages per player
They should have their outer leaves attached and should vary in size from very small to whoppers, and if possible have soil still attached to their roots.

2. Tub of soil or garden trough
This should be large enough to fit the cabbages in – pushed into the soil.

3. Footstool or step
This is for shorter players to reach right down into the trough.

4. Long, soft scarf for use as a blindfold

5. Vegetable knives and a surface to cut the cabbages open on

HOW TO PLAY

✳ Before the start of the game you, the host, should roll the cabbages over the soil and push them down into it.

✳ Ask for a volunteer and put the blindfold on them.

✳ Guide them towards the tub and help them to make contact with the soil with both hands.

✳ They must then say, 'Kind lover, reveal thy nature and thy intent.'

✳ It is important for the player to have a good root around and feel at least two or three cabbages before pulling one out.

✳ They should lightly shake the cabbage over the tub and then rejoin the other players.

✳ The next person puts on the blindfold and chooses a cabbage until everyone has one.

THE RESULTS

These are the meanings players can gain from scrutinising the cabbages they have chosen:

DIRT The amount of dirt still clinging to the roots of the cabbage indicates the future financial status of the prospective partner (much dirt equals much money).

SHAPE AND CONDITION The shape and condition of the cabbage foretells the appearance of the intended; for example a little squat one may indicate a partner greater in intellect than in height. A healthy, well-shaped cabbage is obviously an advantage for players of either sex. Wilting cabbages are not a good omen when referring to a future male lover.

LEAVES The profusion or otherwise of leaves indicates whether there will be many children from the union or just one or two, and how quickly they will arrive.

STALK Have a look at the stalk. The longer and thicker the stalk the more amorous and devoted the lover.

HEART Cut the cabbage open and nibble the heart. A sweet, tender heart reflects the same in a partner. A tough one suggests that the lover will need to be mellowed by softening up. A yellowing heart may indicate a more mature lover.

Be as ingenious as you wish at interpreting the characteristics of other people's lovers and feel free to have a nibble of each other's cabbages.

TIPS *Players shouldn't try for the biggest cabbage as there are lots of other criteria to consider.*

As soon as players feel their cabbage by a tingling in their fingers, they should go for it.

FOLLOW-UP ACTIVITIES

When guests get home they must put the cabbage stalk behind the bedroom door and leave it there until it starts to wilt or smell less than fragrant. By this time they should have met their love. If not, they should plant the stalk in soil in which they have imprinted their footstep and their true love will come within three full moons of the planting.

Before guests leave the party, offer them small pieces of salted fish such as herrings to eat with salted potato crisps. Instruct them not to drink any water before going to bed. Their true love will bring them a drink in their dreams and this way the identity will be confirmed.

If you have enjoyed this game you may also like to try:
The other Halloween Party Games (see pages 124–144)
Christmas Party Games (see pages 145)
New Year Party Games (see pages 169–194)

FORTUNE-TELLING GAMES

What are they?
Three very fast fortune-telling games that are played
in quick succession

Number of players
Any number.

Event
Halloween parties for teenagers and adults of either sex or mixed
sex; New Year and Christmas parties, also girls' nights in and
hen parties.

ABOUT THE GAMES

These are three fun fortune telling methods that are very physical and basic and so ideal for getting everyone talking and laughing, and for kick-starting a slow party or event.

Game 1: Love Come to Me

EQUIPMENT

1. Four dishes or deep saucers
One dish filled with clean water, one with dirty or dark water (add half a drop of dark food colouring), one empty and one filled with small feathers or thin paper streamers from used party poppers.

2. Blindfold

HOW TO PLAY

* The four dishes are arranged in a row on a table.

* One person is blindfolded and the dishes are rearranged several times.

* The player is turned around three times and must say three times:

   Fortune, fortune tell me
   Am I pretty or plain,
   Or am I downright ugly

And ugly to remain?
Shall I marry a gentleman?
Shall I marry a clown?
Or shall I marry old pots and pans
Shouting through the town?

The rhyme can be adapted for male players.

✳ The contestant reaches out with their left hand, if necessary with guidance, until they put their hand in one of the saucers.

✳ The blindfold is then taken off.

✳ The items can be replaced (if necessary) and a new player chosen.

THE RESULTS

If the person touches:

CLEAN WATER Their intended will be of a similar age to them, attractive and available. In the case of an older person the intended may be a charismatic toy boy or girl.

DIRTY WATER Their intended will be older or divorced.

EMPTY PLATE They will remain single until next Halloween.

FEATHERS/STREAMERS They will meet an entrepreneur or adventurer who will either become a millionaire/ess in a short time or will whisk them off to an offshore haven.

TIP Players should relax their fingers and let them be drawn to the correct dish – they shouldn't try to guess.

Game 2: What Shall My Fortune Be?

EQUIPMENT

1. Four plain cups of the same size

2. Ring

3. Silver coin

4. Sprig of heather or small lucky horseshoe

HOW TO PLAY

* You, the hostess, place the ring, coin and heather each under one of the cups and leave the fourth cup empty.

* Invert the cups on a table and mix them around several times.

* The first volunteer is twirled around three times clockwise and three times anti-clockwise while you move the cups further around the table.

* The volunteer touches each of the inverted cups in turn, saying three times, 'Three by three, so shall my fortune be.'

* They then turn over one of the cups and look to see what is under it.

* They return the item to the cup and mix the cups around again.

* The game continues very fast, repeating the same method, until everyone who wishes to do so has picked a cup.

THE RESULTS

The item picked gives a fun 12-month forecast.
RING You will marry within the year or enjoy great love and admiration – or if you are already married have a fun flirtation.
HEATHER/HORSE SHOE You will have unexpected good luck.
COIN Extra money or a promotion is coming very soon.
EMPTY CUP You will need to make your way in the world by hard work over the next year.

TIP Players shouldn't decide in advance which fortune they would like. They may be pleasantly surprised.

Game 3: Mashed Potato Game

EQUIPMENT

1. Set of symbols
Comprising two rings, two silver coins, two round seashells, two buttons, two heart-shaped charms/lockets and two keys. These must be large enough so that the players will not swallow them, and must be washed.

2. Huge bowl of mashed potato

3. Fork, plate and spoon for each player

If more than ten people are playing have a second bowl of potato and another set of symbols, two rings, and so on, for each extra group (up to ten guests per group).

HOW TO PLAY

* Play before people get too merry so they don't swallow anything, and warn everyone to be careful. (Note that the game has been played for hundreds of years without any ill-effects.)

* In advance of the game, put the symbols in the bowl of mashed potato and mix the potato mash around so that they are hidden.

* Dim the lights and get everyone to take a big scoop of mashed potato and put it on their plates.

* They should then sift through the mashed potato to search for any symbols (eating the mash is optional).

* If they can't find a symbol they are allowed one more scoop of mashed potato.

* Some may get more than one symbol in the first attempt and so get a double fortune.

THE RESULTS

This game offers a prediction for the next 12 months. If you find two symbols, the first refers to the first six months ahead and the second to the second six months ahead.

RING You will be happily wed or devotedly admired within 12 months.

COIN You will acquire fame or wealth.

BUTTON You will settle down and maybe have a family.

HEART You will have a passionate love affair or be tempted by an exciting flirtation.

SHELL You will travel to far-off places.

KEY You will have a new home.

NOTHING A secret to your advantage will soon be revealed.

TIP Players shouldn't delve around looking for a symbol; they should let their fate come to them.

FOLLOW UP-ACTIVITIES

Put together all the information from the three games and discuss the predictions.

If you have enjoyed these games you may also like to try:
Christmas Party Games (see pages 145-168)
New Year Party Games (see pages 169-184)
Song of Solomon Love Game (see page 40)

CHRISTMAS
PARTY GAMES

CHRISTMAS EVE
LOVE GAME

What is it?
A traditional love divination game for women of all ages (whether married or not) that goes back to pre-Christian times. It was very popular in Victorian times among young unmarried friends. Amazingly, even sceptics report that it really works.

Number of players
Traditionally three, seven or nine, but any number is fine.

Event
Although often played in the run-up to midnight on Christmas Eve (at around 11 p.m.), it can be played at any pre-Christmas late-night event; also a good girls' night in game at any time of the year. The game is a wonderful antidote to the frantic hype of Christmas.

ABOUT THE GAME

This game either reveals to unattached women their future husband, or for those who are attached, confirms the rightness of their choice.

The women who played the game in the distant past would gather holly and ivy, plus fresh juniper if they could find it, before darkness fell. They would then return to the fireside to decorate the room with holly and ivy boughs, symbols of the king and queen of the Christmas season. Afterwards they would create the love chain that was to be burned (see below), put on white or party dresses, and have supper together away from any men folk before rejoining the men. The game would commence at the stroke of 11 p.m., and only the players would be admitted to the room in which it took place.

EQUIPMENT

This depends on how traditional you wish to be:

1. Open fire or huge red candle

The candle should be embedded in sand placed in a deep, metal fire-proof bucket or sturdy, deep metal pot.

2. Tea lights

Arranged so it is possible to read the prayer book (see below) in the dimly lit room.

3. Holly and ivy

You will want to decorate the room with holly and ivy, but according to what you are using to burn it you will need different methods:

* If using an open fire you will want to weave a love chain. This is entwined holly and ivy strands secured with twine, one strand for each person who is present.

* If using the candle you will need holly and ivy leaves in a dish.

4. Twine

To bind the love chain.

5. Traditional prayer book containing the marriage ceremony

Game in a hurry

Burn alternate holly and ivy leaves in the candle and drop them in the sand as soon as they kindle.

HOW TO PLAY

* When you are all in the room, lock the door and hang or set the key over the mantelpiece.

* Sit around the fire or central candle and work mainly by the tea lights.

* Each person in turn, from youngest to oldest, then pulls or cuts a hair from their head, saying: 'I offer this sacrifice to him most precious in my sight. May he come with wings of flame, and speak to me his own true name.'

* They then cast their hair in the fire/candle in turn.

* If using a fire the oldest person present wraps the holly and ivy chain around a log and puts it on the fire to burn.

* If using a candle the oldest person holds the holly and ivy leaves in turn in the candle flame so that they just catch light at the edges, and drops them into the sand.

* In the meantime the others present open the prayer book at the wedding service pages, and take turns to read the wedding vows over and over again until the chain has burned or all the holly and ivy leaves are gone.

* Any lights are then extinguished, and in the dimness each person will see their future spouse or present lover crossing the room and feel their caress.

TIP Half close your eyes in the dimness and allow an image to build up in your mind – whether it is of your current partner or someone you would like to be with.

FOLLOW-UP ACTIVITIES

Make dumb cakes. Go straight to the kitchen and, using a flapjack or oatcake mix or a traditional recipe (traditionally oats, barley and water, which are a bit tasteless), work in silence with the other women to make a batch of dumb cakes. Each woman should mark the initial of her lover (if known) or a question mark (if unknown) on top of one of the small cakes and bake it in the oven.

At midnight, the kitchen door will open and the spirit double of your true love will come and turn your cake. Each person will see their own love. Since they may appear only in your mind's eye, be sure to set the oven timer for five minutes after midnight to avoid having to send for the fire brigade.

Either eat the cake or, if your lover is in the house, feed it to him.

If you have enjoyed this game you may also like to try:
The other Christmas Party Games (see pages 152-167)
Halloween Party Games (see pages 123-144)
Song of Solomon Love Game (see page 40)

PSYCHIC HERB
DIPPING

What is it?
Traditional party games like this one were first played in pre-Christian times on the Midwinter Solstice around 21 December, when it was believed that the sun or the sun king was reborn. They were very popular from medieval times right through to the Victorian period.

Number of players
Any number.

Event
Any Christmas or pre-Christmas party, whether at work or with friends and family.

ABOUT THE GAME

In medieval times Christmas lasted for 12 days and even ordinary families would have big celebrations. However, even in wealthy homes, many of the gifts were simple and made by hand from herbs and flowers gathered, dried and preserved throughout the year.

The idea of this game is based on the ancient folk meanings of common herbs (given below, see page 155) that when selected from a bran tub (originally bran was used as the filling instead of the sawdust used here) told the fortunes of the people who chose them. They also acted as good-luck charms.

> ## Game in a hurry
> Cut up paper doilies or use Christmas paper to make small twists of herbs secured with ribbon. Use dried cooking herbs; also fragrant herbal tea bags can be split and their contents used.

EQUIPMENT

1. Dried herbs, flowers and spices
You will need a selection of herbs and spices from the list below, although you only need small quantities of each. You can also use dried chamomile flowers from a tea mix and dried lavender from any health shop or gift store. Dried rose petals and other dried flowers are widely available for making potpourri.

153

2. Small drawstring bags, tiny cloth purses or twists of fabric with small ribbon ties

These must be large enough to contain a tablespoon of herbs or flowers, and you will need at least one for each guest. Keep separate types of herb in each bag so you have a sage bag, a lavender bag, and so on. In each bag place a piece of paper with the herb or flower name and the key word (for example, sage wealth) written on it.

3. Tub or barrel filled with sawdust or wood chippings

This is to hold the herb bags.

4. Small tea lights

These should be set around the room.

HOW TO PLAY

* You, the host, must put a teaspoon of one type of herb into each drawstring bag and seal the bags.

* Drop the bags into the tub before the party and have your list from this book ready to give extra information on the different herbs. You can have the original jars close to hand in case any labels fall out.

* Light the tea lights and dim any other lights in the room.

* Starting with the youngest person present, they must delve into the tub, and say, 'Herb of luck, herb of love, herb of health and

joy, bring to me what I do wish, that Christmas I enjoy.'

* They should then name a wish silently and draw out a bag of herbs but not open it.

* This continues until everyone has a herb bag.

* When everyone has a bag the hostess says, 'Merry Christmas to you all,' and counts slowly down from ten. On nought all the bags must be opened at the same time.

THE RESULTS

All the players discover the identities of their herbs and their basic meanings, and the hostess can read out the further information about the herb, spice or flower.

HERB	POWER
Allspice	Money, courage, luck, healing.
Almond flakes	Abundance, prosperity, love without limits.
Angelica (use cake decorations if you can't get the herb)	Banishes hostility from others; protection, healing; promises a golden future.

Anise/aniseed	Makes you young and beautiful/attractive and desirable to others.
Apple blossom, dried as potpourri ingredient or dried apple flakes	Fertility, health, love, long life.
Basil	Love, travel, wealth, conquering fear of flying.
Bay leaves	Protection, psychic powers, healing, fidelity, prosperity, fertility.
Bergamot as pot-pourri ingredient	Money, house moves, career, success.
Carnation	Strength, healing, family devotion.
Catnip	Cat magic, love, beauty, happiness in home, fertility.
Cedar chips	Healing, house moves, money, protection.
Chamomile	Money, quiet sleep, affection, family.
Cinnamon	Spirituality, success, healing powers, psychic powers, money, love, passion.

Cloves	Protection, banishing negativity, increased self-confidence, passion, love, money.
Coconut flakes	Fertility, motherhood, the flow of new life and opportunities, health.
Coriander	Love, health, healing, giving birth to wise and intelligent children, anti-theft and loss of money or property.
Curry mint	Protection against evil and malice, passion, prosperity.
Dandelion (use dandelion tea)	Brings love and long life, also a faithful lover.
Dill	Protection, keeping home safe from enemies and those who have envy in their hearts; also for bringing money, passion, luck.
Fennel	Protection, healing, courage, travel, babies and children.
Fenugreek seeds	Increased prosperity over a period of time, not only in resources but also in health and strength.

Feverfew	Travel opportunities, house moves.
Ginger	Love, passion, money, success, power.
Heather	Passion, loyalty, fertility, long life, good luck.
Hibiscus (found as potpourri ingredient)	Passion, love, skill in divination, self-esteem.
Ivy leaves (keep away from small children)	Protection, healing, married love, fidelity, breaking possessiveness.
Jasmine flowers (found as potpourri ingredient)	Passion, moon magic, money, prophetic dreams.
Juniper berries	Protection, anti-theft, love, banishing negativity, good health, protection against accidents; increase in male potency, new beginnings.
Kelp, seaweed (can buy as powder)	Prosperity, travel overseas or good news from abroad.
Lavender heads	Love, protection (especially of children), quiet sleep, long life, purification, happiness and peace, kindness in relationships.

Lemon balm	Love, success, healing.
Lemon rind, grated	New beginnings, energy, psychic protection, improved memory, employment.
Lemongrass	Repels spite, protection against snakes – reptilian and human – passion, increase in psychic awareness.
Lemon verbena	Purification, love, self-esteem, protection against malice, good for job hunting.
Lilac (found as pot-pourri ingredient)	Cleansing negativity, domestic happiness, contacting old friends and lovers from the past.
Marigold (found as pot-pourri ingredient)	Protection, prophetic dreams, legal matters, increase in psychic powers, increase in love over time.
Marjoram (sweet)	Protection, love, happiness, health, money.
Orange rind or dried blossom (found as pot pourri ingredient)	Love, marriage, abundance, self-confidence, good luck.

Parsley	Love, protection, divination, passion, removing bad habits.
Pennyroyal	Strength, protection, peace, travel; good for business and new jobs.
Peppermint	Money, protection while travelling, purification of bad habits, energy, love, healing, increase in psychic powers.
Pine (collect needles from park or from real Christmas tree)	Healing, fertility, purification, protection, money; returns hostility to sender.
Poppy (found as pot-pourri ingredient)	Fertility, sleep, money, luck, invisibility in a threatening situation.
Rose petals, dried	Love, enchantment of lovers, increase in psychic powers, healing, love and love divination, luck, protection.
Rosemary	Love, passion, increase in mental powers, banishing negativity and nightmares; also for purification, healing, quiet sleep, increasing radiance and charisma, preserves youthfulness.

Saffron	Love, healing, happiness, passion, strength, increase in psychic powers, offers second sight.
Sage	Wealth, long life, wisdom, protection, grants all wishes, improves memory, good health, power of all kinds, leadership.
Sagebrush (break up a small cheap smudge stick)	Purification, banishing negativity, empowerment, promotion.
Spearmint	Healing, love, increase in memory and concentration, protection during sleep, improved job prospects.
Tarragon	Herb traditionally associated with dragons, excellent for courage, new beginnings and overcoming any obstacles; good for insomniacs.
Thyme	Health, healing, prophetic dreams, increase in psychic powers, improvement in memory, prosperity, love, new job, courage.
Valerian	Love and love divination, quiet sleep, fertility, purification, protection against hostility and rivals.

Vanilla	Love, passion, marriage, increase in mental acuity, fidelity, harmony.
Vetivert	Love, breaking a run of bad luck, money, anti-theft, protects against all negativity and jealousy.
Violet (dried – found as potpourri ingredient)	Keeping secrets, uncovering hidden talents, new love, love that cannot be revealed.

TIP Players should wish silently and as they put their hand in the bag, repeat the wish silently three times. They will find that the herbs they choose should relate to the wish.

FOLLOW-UP ACTIVITIES

After examining and discussing the contents, the bags should be refastened and the central candle lit by the oldest person to represent the rebirth of light and hope at Christmas. All other lights should be extinguished, except for the small tea lights around the room.

Everyone then walks in a circle nine times around the candle holding their bag and repeating their wish silently. The candle is blown out by everyone at the same time, and all the players shout out their wishes at the same time. Everyone stands in the darkness, counts to ten aloud and shouts, 'Merry Christmas and may our wishes come true.' The bags are taken home and kept until the fragrance disappears, when the contents are scattered to the winds.

If you have enjoyed this game you may also like to try:

The other Christmas Party Games (see pages 145–168)

Halloween Party Games (see pages 123-144)

New Year Party Games (see pages 169–194)

CHRISTMAS GHOSTS

What is it?
A traditional Christmas ghost story game as an antidote to too much food, hype and television.

Number of players
Any – the more the better.

Event
Christmas night or any festive night. In pre-Christian times the game was played on the night of the Midwinter Solstice (around 21 December). Suitable for family parties of mixed generations, excluding younger children; good for house and hotel parties, and also at New Year and Halloween.

ABOUT THE GAME

Because Christmas and the Midwinter Solstice (the shortest day) are a transition in the year, they are naturally associated with ghosts. In Victorian and Edwardian times, Gothic-style ghost and vampire stories were the staple of family Yuletide parties after supper and after dark.

The idea of this game is that everyone sits around in darkness; a spooky word is chosen at random from the hat by an individual and must be woven into a collective scary story. The only light is that of the small lantern by which to read the words.

EQUIPMENT

1. About 40 different words or phrases on separate pieces of paper

Be as inventive as you like as long as they have a spooky theme. They might include:

Bats	Crows
Black cat with blazing eyes	Deep dark dungeons
Bloody sword	Demons
Bony hand on shoulder	Devil hounds
Bottomless black pool	Eerie green glow
Carriage wheels	Face dripping blood
Caves	Fiery axe
Cellars	Figure walking through wall
Churchyard with open graves	Ghostly horn in the deserted forest
Coffins that spring open	Gothic ruined castle

Groaning from within the earth

Headless horsemen

Hooded figure

Lifeless corpse

Locked doors with no handles

Moving black shadows

Old witch with bony fingers

Poltergeist

Rats

Rattling chains

Screaming

Screech owl

Skeletons

Spectres

Storm

Swirling mist

Toad with jewel around neck

Vampires

Voices on the wind

Werewolf

2. An old top hat or deep black box for holding the slips of paper

3. Single lantern

You can use the type with a glass bulb and a tea light inside, or an electric one.

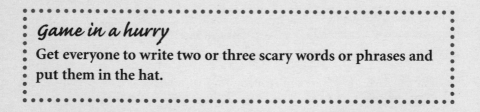

Game in a hurry

Get everyone to write two or three scary words or phrases and put them in the hat.

HOW TO PLAY

✳ Wait until it is late and the house is quiet. Switch off all phones, stereo systems and television sets.

✳ Put all the slips of paper in the hat.

✳ Draw the curtains in the room and extinguish all the lights except for that of the small lantern, which should be placed in the centre of the room.

✳ Everyone sits around in a circle on the floor and in turn the hat is passed around with the lantern. The first person chooses a word or phrase from the hat and starts to invent the ghost story using the word they have chosen.

✳ When they are ready, they leave the story at a crisis point and pass the hat and lantern to the next person. They then take another word and weave that into the story, again ending in suspense.

✳ When the hat has been around the group once, the lantern is extinguished (make sure you know where the light switch is in case anyone panics) and anyone can add to the story at any time without picking words out of the hat.

✳ The game ends when the story comes to a natural conclusion.

TIP Players should be as over the top as they like as this is a Victorian game, so horror and exaggeration are appropriate.

✳ Each person should aim to end their contribution with as high a note of suspense as possible.

FOLLOW-UP ACTIVITIES

Try these Christmas Night rituals to finish the evening on a fun note.

❈ Divide into men and women and have a contest to see who can sing 'The Holly and the Ivy' the loudest. Have a rehearsal first and stand up when you sing. Traditionally, the carol was sung as a competition between the ivy queen and her maidens and the holly king and his men. The sex that sang loudest got to tell the other sex what to do for the rest of the holiday.

❈ Bring out a dish of Christmas cake and describe the following old custom. Walk upstairs backwards eating the piece of Christmas cake and place the crumbs beneath your pillow. You will dream of your true love – or a secret admirer.

❈ Serve baked apples (with cream, of course) and have a bowl of holly sprigs ready. Everyone must take a sprig of holly and put it beneath their bed head in the centre. Traditionally, the holly was sewn or pinned to people's night attire, but this can be a bit hazardous, especially if your guests are merry. Sit up in bed and eat a baked apple and you will talk to your true love (or secret admirer) in your dreams.

If you have enjoyed this game you may also like to try:
The other Christmas Party Games (see pages 145–163)
Past Life Game (see page 20)
Pass the Crystal Ball (see page 86)

NEW YEAR
PARTY GAMES

GAMES FOR BRINGING IN THE NEW YEAR

What are they?
Traditional games to welcome in the New Year and good luck.

Number of players
Any.

Event
New Year's Eve parties for family, friends or acquaintances to tap into the potential and optimism of new beginnings and attract good fortune for the year ahead.

ABOUT THE GAMES

People have always celebrated the turning of the year. One of the places where the New Year is most enthusiastically recognised is in Scotland. The ancient custom of New Year fires to burn out the Old Year has survived there and in other areas with Celtic, Scandinavian and Teutonic influence. The fires purified the New Year, kindled new energies and burned all the old bad luck, and this is recalled now in candle ceremonies.

Feasts were held at this time because if the year began with a good fire and plenty of food, sympathetic magic (in which you could act out what you wanted to happen) decreed that it would continue to yield prosperity and abundance. Nuts and eggs were often given as symbols of the fertility of the coming year.

Bell ringing, the sounding of hooters, cannon fire and fireworks at midnight go back to the primitive belief that malevolent spirits assembled at celebrations, especially at transitions in the year. The noise drove them away. You can, of course, still celebrate with outdoor bonfires and fireworks.

In places influenced by Celtic, Scandinavian and Teutonic customs, all the doors of a dwelling may be opened and then closed just before midnight by the head of the household to let out the bad luck. A dark-haired man, representing the New Year, knocks at the front door at midnight to bring in the New Year and good fortune.

There are two separate New Year's Games in this section. The first involves burning the old calendar, the second bringing in the New Year. The two games run into each other since as you call 'Come in

New Year' in Game 1, the first-footer of Game 2 appears. You can choose one or the other game, but with good stage management you can be starting Game 2 before Game 1 ends. The first game ends at midnight, which is when the second game begins.

Game 1: Candle and Calendar Game

EQUIPMENT

1. Red pen

2. Large single-sheet calendar with squares marking the days
This should show the current year.

3. Large dark-coloured candle in holder
This should be standing on a deep metal tray.

4. Ball of red wool

5. Old metal pot

6. White candle in holder
This should be placed on a deep metal tray.

7. Noisy objects
Such as bells, wind chimes and saucepan lids.

8. Chiming clock, stopwatch or watch

This should be very accurate as timings are crucial.

HOW TO PLAY

❋ Choose who will represent the spirit of the New Year. Traditionally this is a dark-haired male, but of course women can equally bring in the New Year. Dress them in a dark coat and hat – they are the first-footer.

❋ Read the instructions carefully and make sure that everyone playing a key role knows what they are doing and when, and that you have deputies to ensure that the timings go smoothly.

❋ Timing of the start of the game depends on how many people are present. For four to eight people, begin about ten minutes before midnight.

❋ Each person writes down a disaster from the year that they would like to forget. They should use the red pen and write on one of the squares of the calendar to show the correct date. (More than one person can write in a square over the others' messages.)

❋ When this has been done, the youngest male present should light the dark candle (they may need supervision).

❋ The youngest female present then ties up the calendar with the red wool, making nine knots to fasten it.

❋ The oldest male present tears a corner off the calendar and burns it in the dark candle flame, and at the same time everyone says:

Old year turn
Old year burn.
Bad luck, do not return – ever.

Everyone should repeat this nine times as fast as possible.

* The rest of the calendar is then ripped to shreds by any children or teenagers present, or by anyone who feels the old year is all too forgettable. The pieces are thrown in the old metal pot and must be put outside the door before midnight.

* At two minutes to midnight everyone except the first footer gathers around the candle tray and a mother, grandmother or the oldest woman present lights the white candle from the dark one.

* Everyone then counts down to midnight.

* On the first stroke of midnight, everyone blows out the dark candle and shouts: 'Come in New Year. You are welcome.'

* At this point the first footer enters. As they do so, everyone bangs and rattles the noisy objects to get the New Year luck energies flowing in the dwelling. Only then can everyone toast the New Year's health.

* This is where the second game, the First-Footing Game, can overlap.

Game 2: First-Footing Game

EQUIPMENT

1. One copper, one silver and one gold-coloured coin
To bring prosperity to the home and all present.

2. Few wrapped sweets, dried fruits and nuts
To ensure all present will have enough practical resources such as food and fuel and also good health.

3. Two or three symbols of different trades such as a pen, a tiny calculator or a small screwdriver
So all present will have good jobs or a source of income during the coming year.

4. Twist of paper containing two or three dried herbs such as basil, juniper berries, pine needles, sage or thyme
These are traditional cleansers and bringers of health and long life.

5. Small cloth drawstring bag
To hold the items listed above.

6. Large bowl of water

7. Large dark-coloured candle in a holder

This should be standing on a deep metal tray. (You can reuse the candle from Game 1 if you are combining these games.)

8. White candle in a holder

This should be placed on a deep metal tray. (You can reuse the candle from Game 1 if you are combining these games.)

9. Noisy objects

Such as bells, wind chimes and saucepan lids.

10. Three coins or gold-coloured or clear glass nuggets for each person playing

These should be in a dish and symbolise New Year resolutions.

11. Chiming clock, stopwatch or watch

This should be very accurate as timings are crucial.

HOW TO PLAY

* Put the ingredients listed from 1 to 4 in the equipment list in the drawstring bag in advance.

* Choose who will represent the spirit of the New Year. Traditionally this is a dark-haired male, but of course women can equally bring in the New Year. Dress them in a dark coat and hat and give them the drawstring bag. They are the first-footer.

* Five minutes before midnight send the first-footer outside.

* Place the bowl of water next to the dark and white candles.

* As midnight strikes, the person or people inside the house shout, 'Come in, New Year. New Year you are welcome,' and at the same time uses suitable objects to make a noise. (You can join Game 1 at this point.)

* The first-footer enters by the front door holding the drawstring bag.

* He should then go out of the back door, saying, 'Out you go, Old Year. Your time is past.'

* The first-footer comes back in through the back door, shuts it, walks upstairs to the top of the house and then comes back down again, shouting continuously, 'Happy New Year,' or 'May Hogmagog bless the house and all that belong to it, cattle, kin and timbers. In meat, clothes and health of all therein, may fortune abound.'

* He deposits the drawstring bag in front of the candles. The white candle should be lit and the black one unlit.

* The New Year is toasted with everyone in order to make a wish, and bless the house, the people present and the world.

* Each person throws their chosen three coins or nuggets into the bowl of water, one at a time. While throwing each one they make a silent New Year resolution.

* It is important not to throw the water away until 2 January, as you don't want to wash the good luck away on New Year's Day.

On 2 January plant the coins or nuggets under a tree or large bush so luck may grow through the year.

✳ Hide the drawstring bag near the heart of the home, where people gather to relax.

THE RESULTS

Happiness and good luck will remain with the house and all present.

TIPS On New Year's Eve, clear out all old clutter, dust away any cobwebs and sweep last year's luck out of the front door. Put all rubbish outside before midnight.

Make sure you are laughing at midnight on New Year's Eve, as what you are doing when the year turns will influence your happiness and moods for the year.

FOLLOW-UP ACTIVITIES

Play some of the divination games (see pages 181 and 183), or have a firework display or bonfire.

If you have enjoyed this game you may also like to try:
The other New Year Party Games (see pages 169–194)
Psychic Pass the Parcel (see page 67)
What's My Future (see page 91)

GAMES REVEALING WHAT THE NEW YEAR WILL BRING

What are they?
Fun divination games to find out what the future year holds. They follow on naturally from the First-Footing Game (see page 176).

Number of players
Any.

Event
All kinds of New Year's Eve and New Year's Day parties; any age or generation of guests.

ABOUT THE GAMES

Each game offers a traditional form of New Year divination to explore the possibilities of the year ahead. These games, which use the scrying process (see page 87), tap into our own intuitive awareness that the conscious mind cannot access.

The idea of this form of divination is that at transition times such as Halloween, Christmas and New Year the boundaries of time are much more fluid than at other times, so it is possible to speculate more accurately about the future. You aren't summoning up spirits, so there is no psychic or psychological danger.

Game 1: Candle Wax Divination

EQUIPMENT

1. Large clear glass bowl
You may want to have more than one bowl if you have a lot of people taking part.

2. Two brightly coloured candles
These must be wax and have the colour running straight through them. Dyed beeswax candles are particularly good. You may want to use several sets of candles if you have a lot of people taking part.

HOW TO PLAY

✳ Fill the glass bowl with fresh water.

✳ The first guest should ask a question out loud while holding a candle in each hand.

✳ When they have asked the question they should shake the candle wax onto the surface of the water.

✳ They will obtain two images, the first a moving image as the wax flows across the water surface, and then a static one as the wax sets.

✳ All the guests can interpret the images they see in the wax.

✳ The first image shows the action to take and the second is the outcome of that action. So if you asked whether you would travel, you might create a boat, which would indicate journeying over-seas; the second image might be a house, suggesting you might even have the chance to settle abroad as a result of the trip.

✳ You can swirl the water with your finger and obtain several consecutive images. In relation to the travel question you might again get a boat and a house, but also a figure, suggesting you will meet a potential lover abroad and that is why you will stay.

✳ All the guests should have a turn at doing this and for each new guest the bowl should be filled with fresh water.

✳ On pages 197–206 I have provided sample image meanings, but encourage guests to chip in with their ideas – the wilder the better.

Game 2: Herb Scrying

EQUIPMENT

1. Large clear glass bowl

2. Dried cooking herbs

Ordinary mixed cooking herbs are best. The traditional divinatory herbs are parsley, sage, rosemary and thyme.

HOW TO PLAY

✳ Fill the glass bowl with fresh water.

✳ The first guest should ask a question out loud.

✳ When they have asked the question they should drop or shake a small handful of herbs on to the surface of the water.

✳ It's better to add too few herbs rather than too many, as more can always be shaken on to the surface. If someone does add too many herbs by mistake, just tip the water away and start again.

✳ The guest should swirl the water in the bowl and will obtain several images that together answer the question.

✳ All the guests can interpret the images they can see in the herbs.

✳ All the guests should have a turn at doing this, and for each new guest the bowl should be filled with fresh water.

THE RESULTS

If the party is small, you can take turns with a single bowl of water and help interpret each other's images. If the gathering is large, different groups can work with a number of bowls. Try to work with people you don't know very well. Participants shouldn't just go for a basic image, but should mention out loud all the ideas that come into their minds, however unlikely they may seem to them. You can check pages 197–206 for the basic meanings.

TIPS Try the two different forms of divination (wax and herbs) to answer the same question or variations on it.

Encourage players to imagine the images in a context. For example, if they see a boat on a sea, do they feel it is a stormy sea or a calm one, a tropical blue setting or a cold place with icebergs?

Participants should trust their feelings. They are invariably right in divination.

FOLLOW-UP ACTIVITIES

In early times, the first water drawn from a well on New Year's morning was said to bring great fortune and happiness. A modern version of this custom is to turn on the cold tap in the sink as soon as daylight breaks or before you leave the party (whichever is earlier). Run the tap fast so that the water bubbles. Use a new glass and fill it with water. Then drink it straight down without speaking.

This will bring you good luck and also ensure that your words are wise in the coming year.

In the morning or when you leave the party, dance around the nearest tree (12 times clockwise), naming a month for each circuit. This will give you happiness, luck and prosperity all the coming year.

If you have enjoyed these games you may also like to try:
The other New Year Party Games (see pages 169–194)
What's My Future? (see page 91)
Who Will Be a Millionaire First? (see page 107)

LOVE GAMES

What are they?
Games played at the turn of the year that reveal details about love and call love to the players.

Number of players
Any.

Event
New Year's Eve and New Year's Day evening parties, but also any festival night such as Christmas, Halloween and Midsummer; good for girls' nights in and hen nights any time of the year. The first game is more female friendly; the second is for everyone.

ABOUT THE GAMES

Love games were traditionally played at transition times when the dimensions between present and future were blurred.

Both games in this section are based on the power of the mind to attract telepathically the right person to make us happy. They give clues about someone coming into our lives or to identify a person we already know, who may be someone our conscious mind has rejected as a potential lover or just not acknowledged.

If you are in a relationship but having doubts or going through an unsettled patch, these games may confirm that the present match could be the right one after all – or that you need not fear being alone for ever if you leave an unsatisfactory relationship.

The first game is based on an old belief that we all have a spirit double within us, which can be seen psychically by someone who is instinctively drawn to our wavelength.

The second game (see page 191) involves pins and magnets to locate a future love or secret admirer. The concept behind the pin and magnet game is that as the magnet physically draws the pin, so we can psychically draw love using the same power.

Game 1: Love Come to Me

EQUIPMENT

1. *Large clothes airer*

2. Stool or low chair

3. Bowl of rose or lavender water or cologne
You can be medieval and make your own – soak fresh rose petals in water and add a teaspoon of vodka. Leave in a sealed jar for 24 hours, then strain off the petals.

4. Divine food
Pungent cheese with holes, with shortbread or oat biscuits. You can adapt this for cheese haters.

5. Lavender, rose or sandalwood incense sticks
These should be set around the room in holders.

6. Tea lights
People need to be able to see in the room, so the number of lights depends on its size.

7. Sprig of fresh sage for each player
This should be kept in a vase of water outside the room you are playing in.

8. Two or three pieces of each woman's prettiest underwear
Warn guests in advance so they come prepared.

9. Few copies of the Maidens' Prayer

I would suggest having a quick rehearsal at reading through this before the game.

HOW TO PLAY

* Choose a small room to play the game in and prepare it by putting the airer in the centre of the room with the stool in front of it.

* Put the bowl of rose water on the stool.

* Ten minutes before midnight, players should eat the divine food (the biscuits and cheese).

* Five minutes before midnight, light your incense sticks and the tea lights, but make sure they are well away from the airer.

* Bring the sage in the vase into the room.

* The guests should all hold their underwear.

* At precisely midnight, lead your guests (holding their underwear) into the room; as they come in they should take a sprig of sage.

* In turn, each of the guests should arrange their underwear on the airer (in total silence).

* Players then sit in a circle holding their sprigs of sage.

* They must all recite the Maidens' Prayer three times. You can read it from a paper first to lead the others in a chorus.

Sweet Saint Agnes, work thy fast.
Bring me love to always last
Good St Agnes the maiden's friend
This night my own true love, pray send
And finally
I ask of thee
If ever man shall marry me,
That this night
I may him see.

✳ In silence each woman should in turn dip her sage in the bowl of rose water and sprinkle it over her own underwear.

✳ The game ends when everyone has sprinkled their garments with rose water.

THE RESULTS

When each woman sprinkles the rose water on her underwear she will feel her true love's hand over hers guiding her and if she turns around fast, she may catch a glimpse of his identity in his etheric or spirit form.

TIP Players should be open to the possibility of not only seeing their love but at the same time telepathically sending out 'love me' thoughts to a known or unknown lover – even if they are cynical.

FOLLOW-UP ACTIVITIES

At bedtime, players should place their underwear and sage under their pillows and they will see their lovers (or future lovers) in dreams, or wake up with their names on their own lips.

Games 2 : Pins and Magnet Love Game

EQUIPMENT

1. Love incense sticks
These should be in holders. Ylang ylang, any spice fragrance and geranium work well.

2. Tea lights
These are to illuminate the room, so you need to judge how many you will need

3. Very large map
You can use a large-scale map of your own area, or a map of a country or continent. Choose according to who your guests are.

4. Small horseshoe magnets
One for each player.

5. Large box of small, silver-coloured safety pins

6. Suitable love prize
Choose this according to the ages and sensitivities of the players.

HOW TO PLAY

✳ The game can be played at any time after sunset.

✳ Five minutes before the game, light the incense and tea lights.

✳ Spread the map on the floor and give each guest a magnet and a safety pin.

✳ Each guest should hold the magnet in their power hand (the one they write with) and the pin in their other hand (the love hand).

✳ In turn, with their eyes closed, each guest should recite the following, nine times:
Near and far, o'er land and sea
A lover true I call to me.

✳ With their eyes still closed they should throw the pin on the map and then open their eyes.

✳ Wherever the pin lands indicates where their lover will come from.

✳ Once everyone has thrown down their pin, each guest in turn should recite the chant backwards:
Me to call I true lover a
Sea and land o'er, far and near.

✳ If they succeed in doing this, they may remain in the game.

* All those who succeeded should sit around the map with their magnets poised.

* You should scatter any remaining pins in the box over the map, reciting the rhyme (forwards) three times.

* The remaining players should count down from ten to zero. When they reach zero they must pick up as many of the pins as possible, holding the magnet in their teeth.

* If no one can recite the rhyme backwards the magnet session becomes a free-for-all.

THE RESULTS

The winner is the one with the most pins and they win the prize.

TIP As players close their eyes and throw their pins, they should imagine that there is a beam of light guiding them to a particular location. They may at this point have a momentary glimpse of their love in their mind's eye.

FOLLOW-UP ACTIVITIES

You can have fun enquiring about people's backgrounds, especially at a singles' party. The serious Nordic-looking guy may well have an aunt in Sri Lanka, the spot where your pin landed. If not, you can speculate about people you have met in your daily life or plan a holiday to the area indicated.

If you have enjoyed these games you may also like to try:

The other New Year Party Games (see pages 169–190)

Christmas Party Games (see pages 145–168)

Guess My Dark Secret (see page 81)

BIRTH SIGNS

♈ **Aries** (21 March–20 April)
The Ram
Keyword *Assertiveness*
Innovative, enterprising free spirits
with a strong sense of identity;
energetic but self-centred.

♉ **Taurus** (21 April–21 May):
The Bull
Keyword *Persistence*
Patient, reliable, practical, loyal,
concerned with material comfort
and security for self and loved ones,
but can be possessive and materialistic.

♊ **Gemini** (22 May–21 June):
The Heavenly Twins
Keyword *Communication*
Adaptable, intellectual,
scientific/technologically adept,
inquisitive and intelligent, but can
be restless and inconsistent.

♋ **Cancer** (22 June–22 July)
The Crab
Keyword *Sensitivity*
Kind, home-loving and nurturing,
especially towards children; creators
of emotional security, but secretive
and can become overly sensitive to
potential criticism.

♌ **Leo** (23 July–23 August)
The Lion
Keyword *Power*
Courageous, generous, noble, proud
and loyal; born leaders, but need
the adulation of others and can be
occasionally arrogant.

♍ **Virgo** (24 August–22 September)
The Maiden
Keyword *Perfection*
Methodical, meticulous, skilful,
perfectionists, modest and efficient,
but can be critical of self and others
and worry over details.

♎ **Libra** (23 September–23 October)
The Scales
Keyword *Harmony*
Balanced and peace-loving, harmonious, diplomatic with a strong sense of justice, but can be unwilling to make decisions and narcissistic.

♏ **Scorpio** (24 October–22 November)
The Scorpion
Keyword *Intensity*
Psychic, mystical, purposeful, sensual and passionate, but can be vengeful and overly introverted.

♐ **Sagittarius** (23 November–21 December)
The Archer
Keyword *Expansiveness*
Visionaries, seekers after truth and meaning, flexible, open-minded, extroverted, optimistic, natural travellers, but can be very outspoken and may lack staying power.

♑ **Capricorn** (22 December–20 January)
The Goat
Keyword *Prudence*
Cautious, quietly resolute, persistent, conventional and ambitious, with great self-discipline, but can be mean and very inflexible.

♒ **Aquarius** (21 January–18 February)
The Water Carrier
Keyword *Idealism*
Independent, idealistic, intellectual, inventive and humanitarian, but can be emotionally detached and somewhat eccentric.

♓ **Pisces** (19 February–20 March)
The Fish
Keyword *Intuition*
Sensitive, sympathetic, imaginative, intuitive, impressionable and spiritual, but can be self-pitying and easily lose touch with reality.

INTERPRETIONS
OF IMAGES

A

Anchor You're feeling insecure – it's time to touch home base or contact old friends.

Ants There are lots of irritating people in your life who need squashing.

Apples Major fertility symbol or money coming from earlier efforts or investments.

Archangel You're being looked after right now by your guardian archangel, but don't push your luck too far.

Arrow Sudden love or lust that could be reciprocated if you wish.

B

Balloon A wild dream or risky venture may get off the ground if you try soon.

Bed Unless you're feeling amorous, a sign that you need time out from the rat race.

Bees You will receive important family news within a week, probably connected to pregnancy, marriage or a house move.

Birds Travel and also the chance to achieve a special dream or ambition.

Butterfly New beginnings that will bring happiness.

C

Cake Something to celebrate within the month.

Car A short journey brings unexpected pleasure and rewards. Good also for driving test success and favourable insurance claims if you're negotiating right now.

Castle You may need to defend your opinions or your reputation.

Cat You've got secrets and it is best to keep them.

Chimney If the chimney has smoke then good luck or happy family times are coming into your life. If there is no smoke you may feel unwanted and misunderstood by loved ones.

D

Dagger Watch out for back-stabbers and gossips.

Devil You're tempted. It's fine to indulge as long as you keep your eyes open and realise that you can't go on like that for ever.

Dog A faithful friend or lover who will always be there for you needs to know you value them.

Door If it is open then it shows an opportunity for extra training or promotion at work. If it is closed it means it could be time to get yourself noticed.

E

Earrings A gift or offer from a secret admirer who is revealed.

Egg One egg means fertility or a birth. More than one egg means that prosperity comes into your home in a month.

Elephant An influential person will help you with a major project or to overcome an obstacle.

F

Face If smiling, you'll make a new friend. If angry, watch out for a quarrelsome neighbour or colleague.

Fairy A wish will come true within a week or two.

Fire The kindling or revival of passion; also danger from being too outspoken.

Fish A sign of abundance and also unexpected generosity towards you.

Frog A fertility symbol; also a chance to make quick money.

G

Gallows Worried about being caught out or trapped by someone.

Ghost Someone from the distant past will turn up soon.

Giant Being bullied or overruled by officialdom or an organisation, or you're in a stronger position than you realise.

Goat Illicit passion or a chance to over-indulge physically or financially.

H

Heart A symbol of lasting love for all lovers or would-be lovers.

Horse Travel may be unexpected but definitely pleasurable in the near future.

House Home moves of all kinds or solving a long-standing housing problem.

Hunters Good if you are seeking to change jobs or find a better job; it may be further afield, though, than you expected.

I

Icicles, ice floes or ice mountains Time for a bit of peacemaking or to improve a frosty atmosphere with certain relatives; icebergs warn of hidden resentment or jealousy so go in slowly.

Indian (Native North American) Trust your instincts and follow your heart.

Island You may be feeling a bit of a Betty- or Billy-no-mates right now; spend more time with good friends and lighten up.

J

Jam A pot of jam says you should avoid tricky situations or being too liberal with the truth.

Jewels You'll get recognition and maybe a tangible reward for your talents; sometimes a wealthy lover in the offing.

Judge Someone's trying to make you feel guilty. Stick to your guns; don't be fooled by a know-all.

Jug Good health and improved finances unless liquid is pouring from the jug. If the jug is full then you will have a settled financial period.

K

Key The answer to an old problem or a new career opportunity not to be missed.

King An older or more powerful man may assist you in your ambitions; also can mean issues with a father or father figure.

Kite A holiday abroad that will fulfil your dreams or wishes (maybe for romance).

Knot A few minor tangles in your master plan or current relationship; avoid misunderstandings and getting into quarrels over trivialities.

L

Ladder Promotion or a creative opportunity to be seized that will lead to great things.

Lamp A mystery solved or a lost possession found.

Leaves Increased happiness, love or money.

Letter News from afar or someone you lost touch with. Any examination results, written proposals or applications will be successful.

Lighthouse Avoid getting too involved in a friend's tangled life. For yourself an unexpected breakthrough.

M

Magician Watch out for a con artist close to hand.

Mask (party) Someone you know well may reveal an unexpected side to their personality.

Maze/labyrinth Everything a bit confusing at the moment? Keep going as all will become clear very soon.

Mermaid/merman A beautiful woman or attractive man is trying to seduce you with soft words, promises and flattery for their own ends.

Meteor Seize the moment or an opportunity for recognition or your fifteen minutes of fame.

N

Naked figure Shed your inhibitions, jump in at the deep end of life and have fun.

Necklace A deepening love and commitment. A temporary quarrel with someone close can be mended – if you want it to be.

Nest with eggs Home-making – or maybe a surprise invitation from someone who is not the settling kind; also a powerful fertility symbol.

Net Increase in profits or positive results from earlier efforts; beware of getting tangled up in other people's affairs.

Nose An older relative, neighbour or work colleague is trying to interfere in your personal affairs or invade your privacy.

O

Octopus Watch out for a new lecherous colleague or acquaintance who will take a fancy to you; alternatively a present lover may turn possessive or feel jealous.

Old person A long and happy life; good news about the health of an elderly relative.

Olives/olive tree An unexpected holiday abroad; increased prosperity, good health and also the mending of a quarrel not of your making.

Owl A good omen if you are studying or training or would like to be; can be a warning not to make too many impulse buys.

Oyster An open oyster containing a pearl heralds a sudden revelation of unexpressed love, admiration or passion; also money coming to you. A closed or empty oyster shell signifies an irritating person who takes up too much of your time and offers nothing in return.

P

Padlock If open, a chance of unexpected freedom and/or of enjoying a passionate relationship; if closed, a mean friend or relative is not paying their fair share; insist they do.

Pagoda A long, happy journey within the next year; alternatively can mean that you will be given a beautiful present that will increase in value over the years, along with the affection of the giver.

Palm tree Fertility, increased prosperity and maybe a trip overseas – or an exotic lover.

Parrot Avoid gossip and rumour, and watch out for those who present your ideas as their own.

Peacock Show off your talents a bit more; alternatively a vain friend, family member or lover needs a reality check.

Pig A sign of impending extravagance or over-indulgence; however, it can also indicate good luck and unexpected money.

R

Rabbit The ultimate fertility symbol; good for all matters concerning babies, children and family life; also a sign of coming good luck.

Rainbow A new beginning after a quarrel, setback or disappointment; it promises happiness and the fulfilment of wishes; also may mean an unexpected win or success in a competition.

Ram A symbol of male sexual potency; for men and women the ram says that if you go head on to achieve what you want you will succeed. However, watch out for an obstinate person.

Ring Marriage or permanent commitment within six months; for a married person an assurance that love will last for ever.

Rose Romance, love and fidelity, whether you are looking for love or are already in a committed relationship.

S

Sailor You, a close friend or one of your immediate family will marry someone from overseas or in the armed forces before the year is out.

Sea A calm sea indicates a peaceful time ahead. A stormy sea says that you should prepare for an exciting and challenging few weeks ahead.

Shoes A new job or business opportunity that brings change; you may move home, relocate or even decide to work from home.

Snake A symbol of rebirth and new beginnings; also a powerful sexual symbol. A chance also to shed old debts and obligations.

Spiders Spiders are very lucky, indicating good fortune and money. Spiders' webs warn of intrigues and plots around you; don't get caught out by your own departure from the truth.

T

Table A table with food on it is a sign of abundance coming. People around a table signify unexpected visitors within a week. An empty table says you will have a lot of unexpected expenses in the near future.

Tank (fish) Fish in a tank are a sign of money coming into your business or home; an empty fish tank says your enthusiasm for a project or person is draining away, although you may not have acknowledged this.

Telephone A telephone says you will receive an important phone call very soon from someone who has not been in touch for a while who is coming back into your life – or an unexpected offer to visit a relative.

Temple Your psychic and healing powers are emerging; if life is frantic leave the fast lane for a while.

Throne A promotion or help from someone senior or wealthy to help you move closer to achieving an ambition.

U

Ugliness An ugly face or person means you are worried about what other people or one particular person thinks of you; an ugly young woman traditionally indicates an unexpected inheritance.

Umbrella An open umbrella with rain around says you will smile your way through any worries or opposition you are facing; an inside-out or broken umbrella means a friend or family member will break a promise.

Underground Underground caverns or tunnels say you should keep secrets and a low profile for a while and conserve finances and energy for a hectic period a month or two ahead.

Unicorn A very lucky symbol indicating that your secret wish will come true. For men it is a major potency symbol.

Universe Stars and planets tell you to aim high to fulfil a seemingly impossible dream as Lady Luck is with you.

V

Van You'll soon be on the move either business-wise or to a new home, and the move will be advantageous.

Vase A female fertility and sexual passion symbol. If there are flowers in the vase it shows a sudden surge of desire or a temptation.

Village A quiet but happy period with gatherings of friends and family and maybe an unexpected addition to the family.

Violin Harmony in love or the acceptance of someone your family disapproved of.

Volcano A surge of power and opportunity; watch out for bad-tempered people who may resent your success.

W

Wagon An old-fashioned wagon full of hay or harvest crops promises extra resources for you. Another fertility symbol bringing an increase in family members, whether through birth, marriage, remarriage or adoption.

Walls High walls can indicate either protection or exclusion depending on whether you are inside or outside them and whether you want to be there or are trying to escape. What do you feel when you see the symbol and what is going on in your life?

Wasps Beware of a vicious-tongued colleague or neighbour and avoid contact with them whenever possible.

Watch A watch or clock is a reminder that it is time for a change.

Whale A huge undertaking that can be successfully fulfilled; traditionally success in commerce, accountancy, banking or administration.

X

X A cross indicates that you have a critical person in your life, who undermines your judgement or confidence – you should ignore them; alternatively time to get rid of a destructive influence.

Y

Yacht Travel for pleasure. Any obstacles to a holiday such as lack of finance will be unexpectedly removed.

Z

Zebra Time to stand out from the crowd and say what you really think.

Zodiac signs If it is your own sign this indicates sudden luck in money; if you wait your wishes will be fulfilled within the year. If it is not your sign, someone of that sign will play a very big part in your life during the coming months.

Zoo Lots of animals in cages suggest that the instinctive spontaneous part of yourself is being restricted by trying to be available for others' often unreasonable needs.